To Stan,
With warmest regards,
Lew Rockwell
July 5, 2014

Against the State

Thanks so much to the LRC readers who
helped sponsor this book, and special gratitude
to these generous benefactors:

Gary D. Fairman

~

Jeffrey P. Buol, Wayne Chapeskie, Brian Wilton

~

Steven R. Berger, John Cavanaugh,
Vincent Cifello, Stephen Dristas,
Eric Englund, Michael Fox,
Christopher Georgacas, Daniel Hopkins,
Angelo Kelly, Richard J. Kossmann, M.D.
Dr. Donald and Linda Miller, Christopher Morrill,
Matthew and Charlotte Muehleck, Matthew Nolan,
Randy and Virginia Paulsen, Micheal Todd Rice, M.D.,
Charles and Ruth Schisler, David Scutt,
Charles and Lisbeth Sebrell, Kathleen M. Sheridan,
Paul Smith in memory of Dr. Frank Englebert Smith
and Julia Dodd Smith,
Karel Smutny, Jesse Phillips Sousa, Zachary Tatum

Against the State

An Anarcho-Capitalist Manifesto

Llewellyn H. Rockwell, Jr.

LewRockwell.com

LewRockwell.com
P.O. Box 1189
Auburn, Ala. 36831-1189
lewrockwell.com

print edition: 978-0-9904631-0-8
epub: 978-0-9904631-1-5

To Murray N. Rothbard,
Mentor, Teacher, Friend,
Mr. Anarcho-Capitalist

Contents

Preface

"THESE ARE THE TIMES that try men's souls." So said Thomas Paine in *Common Sense*, a pamphlet that sparked the American Revolution. We face similar trying times today. The American government embroils us in destructive, costly, and illegal wars. Under the malign management of the Fed, money and credit are subject to inflationary pressures that, as Austrian business cycle theory explains, lead to depressions. The government subjects us to a crushing tax burden. Our civil liberties are under continued assault, and the government claims the right to kill us without trial. The government's excuse for this is the unnecessary "war on terror." If we didn't intervene abroad, there would be no terrorist blowback against America. In any case, the threat is grossly exaggerated. As if this were not enough, the government also wages a harmful "war on drugs" that puts thousands in jail and discriminates against blacks.

Matters are no better at the state and local levels. The police are supposed to protect us, but all-too-often, they kill us instead. SWAT teams sometimes go to the wrong address on their misbegotten drug raids and then kill and brutalize innocent victims. State and local governments take over our property under "eminent domain." These governments also take away our money through taxation. The state school system has failed miserably. It subjects its young captives to compulsory indoctrination, designed to get them to be pliant to the depredations of the government.

The list could go on and on. These evils are not the product of temporary malfunctions in the state. To the contrary, the state is by nature evil. As Franz Oppenheimer and his disciple Albert Jay Nock showed, the

9

state began in violence and it has always been an instrument of violence. It is a means by which one group in society can exploit the rest of us. St. Augustine said, "Without justice, what is the state but a great robbery?" Without justice — the state by its nature cannot be just.

If this is so, the answer to the problems sketched above is apparent. We must get rid of the state and replace it with voluntary arrangements. Instead of entrusting our protection to a predatory state, why not rely on peaceful cooperation of people in a free market?

Many readers will be tempted to throw up their hands in horror. "This is anarchy," they will say. They are right, but anarchy does not mean what they think it does. Many people think that "anarchy" is a synonym for "chaos." "Mere anarchy is loosed on the world," as Yeats said. This is not what we have in mind. Anarchy is precisely the reverse of chaos. Libertarian anarchists contend that the free market is the best way to produce a peaceful and prosperous social order.

In this book, we will see how an anarchist society will solve our major social problems. Except for small groups of exploiters, we would all be better off if we lived in an anarchist system. In making our case, we will rely heavily on the pioneering work of Murray Rothbard. He combined the best features of Austrian economics and the nineteenth-century individualist anarchist tradition into a uniquely powerful synthesis. In works such as *Power and Market*, *The Ethics of Liberty*, and *For a New Liberty*, he showed how an anarchist system would work.

In order to make the case for anarchism, we have to meet one objection that is likely to occur to many readers. If the state mismanages the economy, oppresses us domestically, and injects us into unneeded wars, why not simply end these bad programs? Why not restore Constitutional, limited government? Isn't anarchism too drastic a response? We will see that this popular answer is inadequate. Government cannot be limited. Further, making the government more "democratic" is no answer either. As Hans Hoppe shows in his contemporary classic *Democracy: The God That Failed*, democracy is part of the problem, not the solution.

We will proceed by first looking in more detail at the disastrous programs the American government is responsible for, and then we will present the anarchist answer to these problems.

INTRODUCTION

WHY I AM AN ANARCHO-CAPITALIST

A GREAT MANY PEOPLE — more than ever, probably — describe themselves as supporters of the free market today, in spite of the unrelenting propaganda against it. And that's great. Those statements of support, however, are followed by the inevitable but: but we need government to provide physical security and dispute resolution, the most critical services of all.

Almost without a thought, people who otherwise support the market want to assign to government the production of the most important goods and services. Many favor a government or government-delegated monopoly on the production of money, and all support a government monopoly on the production of law and protection services.

This isn't to say these folks are stupid or doltish. Nearly all of us passed through a limited-government — or "minarchist" — period, and it simply never occurred to us to examine our premises closely.

To begin with, a few basic economic principles ought to give us pause before we assume government activity is advisable:

- Monopolies (of which government itself is a prime example) lead to higher prices and poorer service over time.

- The free market's price system is constantly directing resources into such a pattern that the desires of the consumers are served in a least-cost way in terms of opportunities foregone.

- Government, by contrast, cannot be "run like a business," as Ludwig von Mises explained in *Bureaucracy*. Without the profit-and-loss test, by which society ratifies allocation decisions, a government agency has no idea what to produce, in what quantities, in what location, using what methods. Its every decision is arbitrary, in a way directly analogous to the problem facing the socialist planning board (as Mises also discussed, this time in his famous essay "Economic Calculation in the Socialist Commonwealth").

In other words, when it comes to government provision of anything, we have good reason to expect poor quality, high prices, and arbitrary and wasteful resource allocation.

There are plenty of other reasons that the market, the arena of voluntary interactions between individuals, deserves the benefit of the doubt over the state, and why we ought not assume the state is indispensable without first seriously investigating to what degree human ingenuity and the economic harmonies of the market can get by without it. For instance:

- The state acquires its revenue by aggressing against peaceful individuals.

- The state encourages the public to believe there are two sets of moral rules: one set that we learn as children, involving the abstention from violence and theft, and another set that applies only to government, which alone may aggress against peaceful individuals in all kinds of ways.

- The educational system, which governments invariably come to dominate, encourages the people to consider the state's predation morally legitimate, and the world of voluntary exchange morally suspect.

- The government sector is dominated by concentrated interests that lobby for special benefits at the expense of the general public, while success in the private sector comes only by pleasing the general public.

- The desire to please organized pressure groups nearly always out-weighs the desire to please people who would like to see government spending reduced (and most of those people, it turns out, want it reduced only marginally anyway).

- In the United States, the government judiciary has been churning out preposterous decisions, with little to no connection to "original intent," for more than two centuries.

- Governments teach their subjects to wave flags and sing songs in their honor, thereby contributing to the idea that resisting its expropriations and enormities is treason.

This list could go on indefinitely.

It's understandable, to be sure, that people may not understand how law, which they assume must be provided in top-down fashion, could emerge absent the state, although there is plenty of good historical work demonstrating precisely this. But if government had historically monopolized the production of any good or service, we would hear panicked objections to the privatization of that good or service. Had government monopolized light bulb production, for example, we'd be told that the private sector couldn't possibly produce light bulbs. The private sector won't produce the size or wattage people want, critics would insist. The private sector won't produce specialty bulbs with only a limited market, since there would be little profit in that. The private sector will produce dangerous, exploding bulbs. And so on.

Since we have lived with private light bulbs all along, these objections seem laughable to us. No one would want any of the scenarios these hypothetical critics warn about, so the private sector obviously wouldn't produce them.

The fact is, competing sources of law have been far from uncommon in the history of Western civilization. When the king began to monopolize the legal function, he did so not out of some abstract desire to establish order, which already existed, but because he collected fees whenever cases were heard in the royal courts. Naïve public-interest theories of government, which no sensible person believes in any other context, do not suddenly become persuasive here.

Murray N. Rothbard was fond of citing Franz Oppenheimer, who identified two ways of acquiring wealth. The economic means to wealth involves enriching oneself by voluntary exchange: creating some good or service for which other people willingly pay. The political means, said Oppenheimer, involves "the unrequited appropriation of the labor of others."

How do we in the Rothbardian camp view the state? Not as the indispensable provider of law and order, or security, or other so-called "public goods." (The whole theory of public goods is shot through with fallacies anyway.) The state, rather, is a parasitic institution that lives off the wealth of its subjects, concealing its anti-social, predatory nature beneath a public-interest veneer. It is, as Oppenheimer said, the organization of the political means to wealth. "The State," wrote Rothbard,

> is that organization in society which attempts to maintain a monopoly of the use of force and violence in a given territorial area; in particular, it is the only organization in society that obtains its revenue not by voluntary contribution or payment for services rendered but by coercion. While other individuals or institutions obtain their income by production of goods and services and by the peaceful and voluntary sale of these goods and services to others, the State obtains its revenue by the use of compulsion; that is, by the use and the threat of the jailhouse and the bayonet. Having used force and violence to obtain its revenue, the State generally goes on to regulate and dictate the other actions of its individual subjects. ... The State provides a legal, orderly, systematic channel for the predation of private property; it renders certain, secure, and relatively "peaceful" the lifeline of the parasitic caste in society. Since production must always precede predation, the free market is anterior to the State. The State has never been created by a "social contract"; it has always been born in conquest and exploitation.

Now if this description of the state is true, and I think we have good reason to believe it is, is merely limiting it possible or even desirable? Before dismissing the possibility outright, ought we at least to consider whether we might be able to live without it altogether? Might the free market, the arena of voluntary cooperation, really be the great engine of civilization we otherwise know it to be?

Let's get back to the Constitution and the Founding Fathers, people say. That would be an improvement, no doubt, but experience has taught us that "limited government" is an unstable equilibrium. Governments have no interest in staying limited, when they can expand their power and wealth by instead increasing their scope.

The next time you find yourself insisting that we need to keep government limited, ask yourself why it never, ever stays that way. Might you be chasing a unicorn?

What about "the people"? Can't they be trusted to keep government limited? The answer to that question is all around you.

Unlike minarchism, anarcho-capitalism makes no unreasonable expectations of the public. The minarchist has to figure out how to persuade the public that even though the state has the raw power to redistribute wealth and fund cute projects everyone likes, it really shouldn't. The minarchist has to explain, one at a time, the problems with each and every conceivable state intervention, while in the meantime the intellectual class, the universities, the media, and the political class combine against him to convey the very opposite message.

Instead of requiring the fruitless task of teaching everyone what's wrong with farm subsidies, what's wrong with Federal Reserve bailouts, what's wrong with the military-industrial complex, what's wrong with price controls — in other words, instead of trying to teach all Americans the equivalent of three graduate courses in economics, history, and political philosophy — the anarcho-capitalist society demands of the public only that it acknowledge the basic moral ideas common to just about everyone: do not harm innocent people, and do not steal. Everything we believe follows from these simple principles.

There is a huge literature dealing with the most frequent and obvious objections — e.g., Wouldn't society descend into violent strife as armed bands fought for turf? How would disputes be resolved if my neighbor chose one arbitrator and I chose another? A short essay can't answer all objections, so I refer you to LRC's anarcho-capitalism bibliography, assembled by Hans-Hermann Hoppe.

There's a joke that's been going around over the past few years: what's the difference between a minarchist and an anarchist? Answer: six months.

If you value principle, consistency, and justice, and oppose violence, parasitism, and monopoly, it may not take you even that long. Start reading, and see where these ideas take you.

1

THE WAR SYSTEM

THE MAIN AIM OF AMERICAN foreign policy is to impose the will of our ruling elite on the rest of the world. In doing so, we have inflicted massive death and destruction, without moral justification. When she was Secretary of State, Madeleine Albright expressed the attitude of the American state elite with chilling clarity. On the *60 Minutes* program, May 12, 1996, Lesley Stahl asked Albright about the economic sanctions the US was imposing on the Saddam Hussein regime in Iraq. Stahl inquired, "We have heard that half a million children have died. I mean, that's more children than died in Hiroshima. And, you know, is the price worth it?" and Albright replied "we think the price is worth it."

Her blatant disregard for human life makes it all the more urgent that we address the question, when, if ever, is a society justified in going to war. One answer is pacifism — war is never justified. This position has much to be said for it, and it is certainly better than our present war-mongering policy. It was not, though, the view that Murray Rothbard adopted. The main problem with absolute pacifism comes out in Hilaire Belloc's lines: "Pale Ebenezer thought it wrong to fight/ But Roaring Bill (who killed him) thought it right." If someone directly attacks you, you may have no alternative to fighting back.

Fighting back — that is the key to Rothbard's position. Unless we are subject to direct attack, war is not justified. The upshot is that war is almost never morally acceptable. Here Rothbard followed the just war tradition, developed by St. Augustine, St. Thomas Aquinas, and later thinkers such as Francisco Suarez and Hugo Grotius.

Cardinal Charles Journet, in his *The Church of the Word Incarnate*, remarked: "After reading this specification [of the conditions for a just war] we might well ask how many wars have been wholly just. Probably they could be counted on the fingers of one hand." The great Catholic theologian and Murray Rothbard entirely agree on this point. For Rothbard,

> There have been only two wars in American history that were, in my view, assuredly and unquestionably proper and just; not only that, the opposing side waged a war that was clearly and notably unjust. Why? Because we did not have to question whether a threat against our liberty and property was clear or present; in both of these wars, Americans were trying to rid themselves of an unwanted domination by another people. And in both cases, the other side ferociously tried to maintain their coercive rule over Americans. In each case, one side — "our side" if you will — was notably just, the other side — "their side" — unjust. To be specific, the two just wars in American history were the American Revolution, and the War for Southern Independence.

As if this were not enough to condemn war, we also need to take account of the new condition posed by nuclear weapons.

> Pius XII condemned "aggressive wars" (using that term in a technical sense, to mean wars of reparation or punishment), and John XXIII condemned wars of reparation: "It is hard to imagine that in the atomic era war could be a fit means to restore violated rights."

How does current American policy stack up against the traditional just war requirements, interpreted in Rothbard's way? To say, "not very well" would be an understatement. Let's first look at the Iraq War, which George Bush began in 2003. Why did the United States get involved?

One of the key reasons was pressure from a group that has come to exercise more and more influence on American foreign policy — the neocons. Paul Wolfowitz, William Kristol, Robert Kagan, and a number of others were not satisfied with American foreign policy. They disclosed their plans in an important book by Kristol and Lawrence Kaplan, *The War Over Iraq: Saddam's Tyranny and America's Mission*, published in

2003. These neocon authors said that foreign policy must avoid "realism." The realists favored working within the balance-of-power tradition of European diplomacy. "This in turn led to the realists' key recommendation: A state must limit itself to the protection of its 'vital interests,' lest it disrupt the balance of power."

A foreign policy realist will not hesitate to ally, if conditions require it, with an undemocratic state, but this strikes at the heart of Kaplan and Kristol's ideas. The key to their approach is that America should embark on a worldwide crusade for democracy. To do so, they claim, will result in a world at peace.

They contend that the "strategic value of democracy is reflected in a truth of international politics: Democracies rarely, if ever, wage war against one another." Given this premise, isn't the conclusion obvious? If only we establish democracy everywhere, the millennium is at hand.

Democracy should be spread worldwide, but one area is the most important for the neocons — the Middle East. Kaplan and Kristol hate all of the political systems of the Arab world, and they propose to replace them: "There is today not a single Arab state that qualifies as a democracy. ... But promoting democracy in the Middle East is not a matter of national egoism. It has become a matter of national well-being, even survival."

In particular, the royalist government of Saudi Arabia must go. Why not replace it as an American ally with a democratic Iraq? "Iraq's experience of liberal democratic rule in turn could increase the pressure already being felt by Teheran's mullahs. ... Iraq could even replace Saudi Arabia as the key American ally and source of oil in the region."

America should therefore strike at Saddam Hussein — remember, they wrote before the invasion began. Incredibly, Kaplan and Kristol predicted that the Iraqis would welcome us with open arms. Then we could start preventive wars against other dictatorships.

> In international law, in international practice and in American history, there is ample precedent for the doctrine of preemption. ... The origins of this concept date back to the father of international law, Hugo Grotius, who in the seventeenth century wrote, "It is lawful to kill him who is preparing to kill."

Of course, we know now that Bush and his administration lied about the "weapons of mass destruction." No one was able to find them, and Bush later had the extreme but characteristic bad taste to lie about this. But an important point is often overlooked. Even if the stories about the weapons had been true, they would not have justified an American preventive war to get rid of them.

Why not? Oliver O'Donovan, one of the leading moral theologians in the Church of England, calls to our attention a vital point. If we take account of his insight, we can grasp immediately why the invasion of Iraq is an unjust war.

O'Donovan, a scholar of great learning, cites a passage from Hugo Grotius that makes clear how classical just war theory responds to our question:

> Grotius allowed defensive war against *inuria non facta*, "wrong not perpetrated," though with this strict qualification: The danger must be immediate ... those who accept fear of any sort as a justification for preemptive slaughter are themselves greatly deceived and deceive others.

As for "democratic peace theory," international relations scholar Christopher Layne remarks,

> The democratic peace theory is probably the most overhyped and undersupported "theory" ever to be concocted by American academics. In fact, it is not a theory at all. Rather it is a theology that suits the conceits of Wilsonian true believers — especially the neoconservatives who have been advocating American Empire since the early 1990s.

What has been the result of our efforts to bring to Iraq the "benefits" of democracy? There's one thing Americans don't talk about: the lives of Iraqis, or, rather, the deaths of Iraqis. It's interesting because we live in an age of extreme multiculturalism and global concern. We adore international aid workers, go on mission trips abroad, weep for the plight of those suffering from hunger and disease, volunteer in efforts to bring plumbing to Ecuador, mosquito nets to Rwanda, clean water to Malawi, human rights to Togo, and medicine to Bangladesh.

But when "we" cause the calamity, suddenly there is silence. There is something odd, suspicious, even disloyal about a person who would harp on the deaths of Iraqis since the US invasion in 2003. Maybe a person who would weep for Iraq is really a terrorist sympathizer. After all, most of the deaths resulted from "sectarian violence," and who can stop crazed Islamic sects from killing each other. Better each other than us, right?

Well, it's about time that we think about the numbers, even though the US military has decided that body counts are not worth their time. Here is the grisly bottom line: more than one million people have been murdered in Iraq since the US invasion, according to Opinion Research Business, a highly reputable polling firm in the UK. Yes, other estimates are lower, but you have to be impressed by what they have found. It seems very credible.

In Baghdad, where the US presence is most pronounced, nearly half of households report having lost a family member to a killing of some sort. Half the deaths are from gunshot wounds, one-fifth from car bombs, and one-tenth from aerial bombs. The total number of dead exceeds the hugely well-publicized Rwandan genocide in 1994.

Aside from the astonishing detail, what jumps out at me is the number of dead who are neither Sunni nor Shia. It is also striking how the further geographically you move from US troop activity, the more peaceful the area is. Americans think they are bringing freedom to Iraq, but the data indicate that we are only bringing suffering and death.

If you have ever lost a family member, you know that life is never the same again. It causes every manner of religious, social, and marital trauma. It's bad enough to lose a family member to some disease. But to a cold-blooded killing or a car bomb or an airplane bomb? That instills a sense of fury and motivation to retribution.

So we are speaking of some 1.2 million people who have been killed in this way, and that does not count the numbers that were killed during the invasion itself for the crime of having attempted to oppose invading foreign troops, or the 500,000 children and old people killed by the US-UN anti-civilian sanctions in the ten previous years.

The US has unleashed bloodshed in Iraq that is rarely known even in countries we think of as violent and torn by civil strife. It is amazing to think that this has occurred in what was only recently a liberal and civilized country by the region's standards. This was a country that had a problem with immigration, particularly among the well-educated and talented classes. They went to Iraq because it was the closest Arab proxy to Western-style society that one could find in the area.

It was the US that turned this country into a killing field. Why won't we face this? Why won't we take responsibility? The reason has to do with this mysterious thing called nationalism, which makes an ideological religion of the nation's wars. We are god-like liberators. They are devil-like terrorists. No amount of data or contrary information seems to make a dent in this irreligious faith. So it is in every country and in all times. Here is the intellectual blindness that war generates.

Such blindness is always inexcusable, but perhaps more understandable in a time when information was severely restricted, when technological limits actually prohibited us from knowing the whole truth at the time. What excuse do we have today? Our blindness is not technological but ideological. We are the good guys, right? Every nation believes that about itself, but freedom is well served by the few who dare to think critically.

The American project of bringing a free society to Iraq could not possibly have worked. Why not? Because a free society requires a free market, and the American regime of conquest was founded on socialist planning by the state.

So you thought that the US went into Iraq to uproot a dangerous dictator and establish democracy? Well, the US military has taken on a job a bit more difficult than that. It is trying to build an economy, which no state in the history of the world has been able to do without the assistance of a vibrant market.

Fallujah, Iraq, has no economy to speak of. The US bombed all that away a few years ago. It doesn't have clean water. The place is filled with rubble. There is some electricity, for about four hours a day, but you can't count on it nor even which four hours of the day it will be. You only need to think for a moment what your life would be like under those conditions.

The US military has taken responsibility for the rebuilding effort, as they have done all over Iraq, where 90 percent of projects have been delayed and delayed. But in Fallujah, the US is promising that by the fall, 80 percent of homes will have clean water. Most implausibly, the US is promising to bring wireless internet to everyone. Just don't drink the water while you surf the web.

How much is this going to cost? Oh, a couple hundred million. Or maybe a few billion. We'll let you know once it's done.

Water distribution relies on electricity, and the US has somehow not been able to get the generating plants working right to make the electricity available. People buy their own generators, but those require gasoline. There is a shortage of gasoline owing to several factors: the masters of the universe who overthrew Saddam have not been able to process the oil from the ground and get it to market, and the gas that is available can only be sold at an ultra-low and controlled price. The US enforces these controls by arresting black-market gas dealers.

Now, there are general and specific problems with the central planning that the US is doing in Iraq. The general problem afflicts all socialist planning. Think of Stalin's plan to bring electrification to the Ukraine, a "progressive" move not unlike Bush's plan to modernize Iraq. It was one disaster after another, all backed by political despotism and death.

Why does socialist central planning not work? The means of production are not held privately, so there cannot be any exchange markets for them and therefore no exchange ratios established. That means there is no way to calculate profit and loss. Without profit and loss, there is no way to assess the tradeoffs associated with alternative uses of resources. That means there is no economy in the literal sense of that term.

Let's say there is only a limited amount of gasoline. Should it be used to fuel trucks to haul debris away, run construction equipment to put in power plants, or used to move building materials in for new schools and roads? There is no way to assess the relative merit of these choices. The same is true for every resource. What is the priority? It ends up being an arbitrary decision by the central planners. In this case, that arbitrariness ends up with Fallujah residents who can view home videos on Youtube but can't get a drink of water without acquiring a deadly infection. The analogy with the Ukraine is unavoidable: electrification in the midst of famine.

The pricing problem, or the calculation problem, as Ludwig von Mises called it, will always and everywhere doom any attempt to centrally plan.

It even makes it impossible to carry out projects from the first to the last stage of production, since every economic good requires many stages of production. After all, even with all of Stalin's secret police and armies, there was nothing they could do to produce a decent crop of grain. The process of production is too complicated to be run by anything as stupid as a government bureaucracy.

The specific problems of martial-law central planning are tied to the way the US has chosen to do business. The government has contracted out most of its work to private corporations. Of the $18 billion that the US Congress has allocated since 2003, 90 percent has been farmed out to private contractors.

This may (or may not) increase efficiency but this strategy does not overcome the calculation problem. The question of what should be built and how much and by when (the core of the economic problem) is still made by the government, not by private enterprise. The contracting agency does not own or sell what it builds. It is there only to do what it is told and pick up the check.

So the "privatization" of construction in Iraq is not a step toward market economics, contrary to what the right says (in praise) or the left says (in condemnation). It only ends up adding another layer of problems, namely the problem of graft and corruption that comes from the decision-making process of who or what is going to get the money.

Mises wrote in 1920 that he could confidently predict the future of Soviet socialism:

> There will be hundreds and thousands of factories in operation. Very few of these will be producing wares ready for use; in the majority of cases what will be manufactured will be unfinished goods and production goods. All these concerns will be interrelated. Every good will go through a whole series of stages before it is ready for use. In the ceaseless toil and moil of this process, however, the administration will be without any means of testing their bearings. It will never be able to determine whether a given good has not been kept for a superfluous length of time in the necessary processes of production, or whether work and material have not been wasted in its completion.

Despite these economic problems in the occupation of Iraq, and despite the horrendous costs of the Iraq War, don't the neocons and the

American policymakers deserve credit for ousting the tyrannical government of Saddam Hussein? No, they don't — they simply replaced a homegrown tyranny with a foreign one.

Query: what lesson has mass death, destruction, bloodshed, and all-around living hell taught the US government about its war in Iraq? Nothing. Or barely nothing. Or maybe just a little bit of something. In any case, it needs to learn that the US is not necessarily God on Earth, and that there is some limit to what rivers of blood can accomplish.

The following words are dated December 22, 2004, and appeared in the *Wall Street Journal*:

> The audacious attack on a U.S. military base in Iraq yesterday that left at least 22 dead, including 15 U.S. soldiers, reignites a simmering debate over whether the large U.S. presence is becoming an impediment to progress toward a stable government there. ... [T]here has been growing sentiment among some senior military officials that the large U.S. presence in the country is helping fuel the insurgency it is intended to combat. These officials argue that U.S. troops might be undermining the legitimacy of the interim Iraqi government and creating the impression that an unpopular occupation will continue indefinitely.

Now, a comment like this can only astound anyone with a clear head about the Iraq war. This bloodshed began in 2003, and only after two years were a few hesitatingly suggesting the incredibly obvious. The War on Terror began even before 2003, a war that might as well have been designed to increase terrorism and confirm the view of those who have concluded that the US threatens the world.

But those who are shocked to read my paragraph above, who regard it as somehow controversial to suggest that the war is having the opposite effect of its supposed intent, to realize that the US presence is not a liberating force but a destabilizing one, to conclude that progress is being inhibited rather than furthered by the occupation, these people are sadly caught up in what can only be considered intellectual delusion.

And yet, this is precisely where the American establishment, particularly its conservative wing, finds itself. They have been unwilling to believe that displays of force will not cause the population to submit. They have blamed all war errors on too little bloodshed and destruction rather than too much. Their constant advice has been to kill more, destroy more, show ever more resolve, and be ever less squeamish about the innocents killed.

What historical parallels exist to those who believed that this war would liberate, pacify, and inspire a region to embrace liberty? One thinks of the Roman armies marching and killing in the name of civilization. And yet the parallel isn't quite there, because Roman imperialism lacked an ideological basis that leads to fanaticism of the type on display here. A better parallel would be the Bolsheviks, who were convinced that the new dawn would arrive once the capitalist class and their offspring were wiped out.

It is true that many supporters of the Iraq War are simply power-mongering liars and sadists who appreciate how the war keeps them and their patrons at the controls. Other supporters come from the class of merchants who stand to benefit from reconstruction contracts and sales of war-related products (though it is becoming increasingly difficult to find private enterprises willing to take the risk in Iraq).

And yet, I continue to believe that what is at the root of all the problems is intellectual error. Something at the heart of American culture leads us to believe that everyone in the world would be pleased to be ruled by us. We seem to have great difficulty in sympathizing with the victims of US foreign policy. In addition, the whole of modern life seems to teach us that force is the answer to all problems. This is the basis of all domestic policy as recommended by both right and left. The Iraq War is nothing but an extension of this model.

The problem with this intellectual error is that it is constantly bumping into the reality of free will. All human beings everywhere in the world have within themselves the capacity for independent thought. They can decide on their own whether they want to obey their masters or take the risks inherent in revolt. They may pretend to obey, but then challenge authority when an opportunity presents itself. People can be very creative about finding ways around the most well-constructed central plan, outsmarting those with the biggest guns by doing the very thing that the powerful least expect.

There are many reasons why tyranny cannot last, but this is the core one. Of course there are degrees of tyranny. People will put up with a lot, as Jefferson observed, before they will take the risk of revolt, especially if that risk implies the certainty of death.

There are also different forms of tyranny. There is *tyrannus in regimine*, a home-grown despot who comes to power through (more or less) legitimate means and then begins to abuse that power and oppress people. If the *tyrannus in regimine* plays his cards right, he can pay off enough and protect enough interest groups to stabilize his rule. In terms of prudence, it might be better to put up with him than to overthrow him — at least this is what Jefferson taught.

The second kind is the *tyrannus in titula*. This is one who takes control through conquest or usurpation. In terms of degrees of legitimacy, this type is the most objectionable and the one most moral to resist, at least according the Western tradition of political thought from St. Thomas through Jefferson.

Rule by military conquest is the prime example of *tyrannus in titula*. It is completely consistent with Western principles to resist, precisely as many are doing in Iraq.

Far from hating our values and hating our freedoms, their resistance is actually a sign that they have embraced a prime value of ours (throwing off the usurper). Whether they are doing so to bring about an Islamic dictatorship, a secular strongman, a complete breakdown of the nation, or democratic freedom, we cannot know. But the principle that drives the resistance is a simple one: the *tyrannus in titula* is always subject to removal.

The main argument that war supporters use to justify what is going on runs this way: military occupation and martial law are awful, but far worse would be rule by Saddam. The first answer simply observes that choices should not be so constrained, any more than Poland should have to choose between being ruled by Hitler or Stalin. A third option of freedom itself should never be ruled out. A second answer observes that a *tyrannus in regimine* has more legitimacy by its very nature than a *tyrannus in titula*, which will always be resisted.

It should not require such an explanation to demonstrate that people are naturally disinclined to appreciate rule by foreign masters. Even Bush once granted this: "They're not happy they're occupied. I wouldn't be happy if I were occupied either."

Robert Higgs has subjected the "humanitarian" case for the Iraq War, unfortunately professed by some self-styled libertarians, to withering scrutiny.

According to the argument Higgs rejects, the justification of the Iraq War does not rest on the supposed presence of WMD. Humanitarian considerations supported the overthrow of the tyrannical regime of Saddam Hussein. True enough, the American invasion has killed innocent people.

But their deaths have been accidental, and these must be weighed against those who would have suffered and died had Saddam's government continued in power.

Higgs rejects completely this sort of moral calculation.

> In the present case, making such a judgment with anything approaching well-grounded assurance calls for powers that none of us possess.

> How does anybody know, for example, what the future harms caused to innocent parties by Saddam or his henchmen would have been, or that those harms, somehow properly weighted and discounted, would be greater than the harms caused by the U.S. armed forces in the invasion of Iraq?

If these calculations cannot be carried out, how can we determine the morally proper course of action? One thing we can know is that we ourselves should not directly kill or injure the innocent; but this is just what the U.S. has done in Iraq.

> Scattering cluster bomblets about areas inhabited by civilians ... was inexcusable: doing so was in no sense necessary to oust Saddam's government. Nor was the use of very high-explosive bombs (two thousand pounds and bigger) in densely populated urban areas a means one can defend morally.

How can defenders of the Iraq War maintain that these deaths were accidental?

> When U.S. forces employ aerial and artillery bombardment — with huge high-explosive bombs, large rockets and shells, including cluster munitions — as their principal technique of waging war, especially in densely inhabited areas, they know with absolute certainty that many innocent people will be killed. To proceed with such bombardment, therefore, is to choose to inflict these deaths.

If the humanitarian argument fails, the claim that Iraq threatened America fares even worse. Who can seriously believe that a nation long subjected to a devastating blockade and bombing posed a danger to America? In the months that preceded the invasion, much was made of Saddam's supposed plans to obtain nuclear weapons. Of course we now know that the intelligence reports that alleged such plans were false. But even if they had been true, an Iraq with nuclear arms was a minor matter.

> [N]otwithstanding the tens of thousands of Soviet nuclear warheads and their sophisticated delivery vehicles kept in constant readiness, the United States was not "blackmailed" by the USSR. Odd that the United States should quake at the prospect of a single Iraqi softball of fissionable material.

After Higgs disposes of the threadbare arguments in favor of the Iraq War, Higgs asks a fundamental question: why should we believe that the Bush administration sincerely intended them? Not only the Iraq War but also the entire "war on terrorism" seems a made-up affair, designed to frighten the American public into support for a foreign policy of military aggression.

Higgs uses a simple and telling argument to show that the campaign against terror is bogus. If we really were in danger, isn't the government doing far too little to protect us?

> If semi-organized gangs of suicidal maniacs numbering in the thousands are out to kill us all, the government ought not to be fiddling with kindergarten subsidies and the preservation of the slightly spotted southeastern screech owl. It ought to get serious.

Fortunately, the difficulties America encountered in making Iraq safe for democracy have slowed the neocons from putting all of their plans for war into effect immediately. But let's not forget about the war in Afghanistan. Here again America got into a war that could have easily been avoided, in order to promote "regime change." John Quigley has a good discussion of the main issues in his book *The Ruses for War*. Supporters of the war said that we "had" to invade in order to seize Osama bin Laden, who was responsible for the 9/11 attacks on America. Quigley shows that this view rests on dubious assumptions. First, when the United

States demanded that Afghanistan surrender bin Laden, it ignored customary procedures of international law.

> The normal international procedure for the surrender of a suspect is extradition. The government that seeks surrender provides information to show probable cause that the person sought committed a crime. A court in the country from which extradition is requested hears the evidence in open court and decides whether there is sufficient evidence that the accused person committed the crime in question. In requesting evidence, the Taliban was thus adhering to accepted international standards.

Instead, the United States demanded that the Taliban surrender bin Laden and other al Qaeda leaders without the customary procedures; when the Taliban did not comply invasion followed. The Taliban said it was willing to negotiate over the conditions for surrender of the suspects, but the US would not discuss its ultimatum. If the Taliban was not sincere, this could soon have been determined, but the US would not wait. As Quigley aptly notes, military force is supposed to be the last resort in a crisis, not the first.

In response, supporters of the war will say that the Taliban regime harbored al Qaeda. But this does not answer our question. Why is the United States justified in doing more than directly attacking the group that assaulted it? From the fact that al Qaeda had bases in Afghanistan, it does not follow that the Taliban forces aimed to aggress against America. Weren't they largely oriented inward, aiming to establish their peculiar vision of an Islamic society? At most, the United States would seem to be justified in measures against Taliban forces that came to the military assistance of al Qaeda.

Even if you accept the mistaken claim that the evils of the Taliban regime justified an American crusade against it, the results for the people of Afghanistan have been terrible.

The US media portrayed the Afghan operation as an extension of the civil rights struggle of the 1960s. US war propaganda picked up the theme and ran with it. An astute observation from Justin Raimondo of Antiwar.com:

> It's interesting, too, how the rhetoric of the Afghan "liberators" and their Western supporters so closely resembles that of the Soviets at the

time of the Russian invasion. The Russians claimed that they were liberating women, bringing education, and Western enlightenment to Afghanistan's medieval darkness: they, too, claimed to be agents of modernity.

If you read Antiwar.com you would have seen the following and please note the contrast with the silly network spin that the liberation of Afghanistan is all about rock music, shaved chins, and short dresses.

Reports the *Times*:

> Northern Alliance forces have threatened to massacre up to 6,000 foreigners fighting with the Taliban in the besieged province of Kunduz. Local fighters would be given a chance to surrender, but Alliance commanders said they had given their troops explicit orders to shoot every foreign fundamentalist — including a handful of British Muslims — among the enemy ranks.

We learn from this Scottish story that:

> A leading Afghan refugee has called on Britain and America to save his homeland from the "rapists and gangsters who have stormed to power in his home country. Mohammad Narveen Asif, who fled Afghanistan two years ago for refuge in Glasgow, voiced concern that one evil has gone and another evil has come to take its place." ... "I think almost every Afghan is happy to see women throwing off the burqa and the Taliban driven out, but the country has now fallen to a bunch of rapists and gangsters."

Another *Times* story reports that the Northern Alliance trapped 700 Taliban men in a school and crushed them with tanks. "Three days later Red Cross workers were still in the ruins taking out bodies."

Finally, it appears that the US campaign in Afghanistan has effectively restored some of the most feared warlords, including known communist murderers, anti-Western Islamic maniacs, and even bin Laden supporters.

Unfortunately, American policymakers have not learned the bitter lessons of Iraq and Afghanistan — did you really expect them to? America seems intent on bringing down the government of Iran. Our sanctions policy carries with it a grave risk of war. Ron Paul, the greatest Congressional champion of liberty, has stated the essentials:

I would like to express my concerns over the Iran Threat Reduction Act of 2011 and my opposition to it being brought to the Floor for a vote. Let us be clear on one critical matter: the sanctions against Iran mandated by this legislation are definite steps toward a US attack on Iran. They will also, if actually applied, severely disrupt global trade and undermine the US economy, thereby harming our national security.

I am surprised and disturbed that the committee viewed this aggressive legislation to be so bipartisan and uncontroversial that a recorded vote was not even called.

Some may argue that we are pursuing sanctions so as to avoid war with Iran, but recent history teaches us otherwise. For how many years were sanctions placed on Iraq while we were told they were necessary to avoid war? Thousands of innocent Iraqis suffered and died under US sanctions and still the US invaded, further destroying the country. Are we safer after spending a trillion dollars or more to destroy Iraq and then rebuild it?

These new sanctions against Iran increasingly target other countries that seek to trade with Iran. The legislation will severely punish foreign companies or foreign subsidiaries of US companies if they do not submit to the US trade embargo on Iran. Some 15 years after the Iran Sanctions Act of 1996 failed to bring Iran to its knees, it is now to be US foreign policy to threaten foreign countries and companies.

During this mark-up one of my colleagues argued that if Mercedes-Benz wants to sell trucks to Iran, they should not be allowed to do business in the United States. Does anyone believe this is a good idea? I wonder how the Americans working at the Mercedes-Benz factory in Tuscaloosa County, Alabama would feel about banning Mercedes from the United States. Or perhaps we might ask the 7,600 Americans who work in the BMW factory in Spartanburg, South Carolina how they would feel. Should the American consumer be denied the right to purchase these products? Is the United States really prepared to take such aggressive and radical action against its NATO ally Germany?

Likewise, the application of the sanctions in this legislation would have a dramatic impact on US commercial and diplomatic relations with Russia and China, who both do business with Iran. It would impose strong sanctions on these countries and would prohibit foreign business leaders — and their spouses and children — from entering the United States. Do we want to start a trade war — or worse — with Russia and China?

The Iran Threat Reduction Act authorizes what will no doubt be massive amounts of US taxpayer money to undermine the Iranian government and foment another "Green Revolution" there. We will establish and prop up certain factions over others, send them enormous amounts of money, and attempt to fix any resulting elections so that our preferred candidates win. Considering the disturbing aftermath of our "democracy promotion" operations in places like Egypt, Iraq, Libya, where radical forces have apparently come out on top, it may be fair to conclude that such actions actually undermine US national security rather than bolster it.

Sanctions do not work. They are precursors to war and usually lead to war. They undermine our economy and our national security. They result in terrible, unnecessary suffering among the civilian population in the target countries and rarely even inconvenience their leaders. We must change our foreign policy from one of interventionism and confrontation to cooperation and diplomacy. This race to war against Iran is foolhardy and dangerous. As with the war on Iraq, the arguments for further aggression and war on Iran are based on manipulations and untruths. We need to learn our lesson and reject this legislation and the push for war.

Obama threatens Iran but this is not enough for him. He helped unseat the government of Libya. Following the US-lobbied UN authorization of military murder in Libya, the death-dealing regime of Colonel Gaddafi said immediately that it would stop all killing. That put Obama's war on hold, for a little while. The crazy Colonel has learned a thing or two about American foreign policy. If you pretend to favor the stated goals of the empire and comply with its stated dictates, you can otherwise do what every government in the world is structured to do: stay in power at all costs.

Gaddafi learned this lesson about a decade ago, when, with much fanfare, he announced that he would stop his nuclear weapons program and join the war on terror. The US then decided to rank him and his regime among the world's good guys, and proceeded to hold him up as an example of wise statesmanship. Then he proceeded to dig in more deeply and tighten his despotic control over his citizens, all with the implied blessing of the US.

But this time it may not work. For weeks, American officials decried Gaddafi's bloody attacks on his people, but does the US really have a problem with dictatorship of his sort? This fact is unknown to Americans, but in the Middle East, and in Arab nations in particular, American commercial interests are regarded as a force for liberation but not the US government. The US has been the key to the power of Middle East dictatorships for decades, among which are Saudi Arabia, Jordan, and Yemen. I leave aside the killing of hundreds of thousands of Iraqi civilians to liberate them.

So it is something of a joke that the US would push a war against Libya in order to save that country from dictatorship. More likely, the real issue here is the same one that inspired the wars against Iraq: the ownership and control of the oil. And even if freedom were the driving motivation, when in modern history has war ever actually brought that to people? All war by nation-states today ends in massive civilian deaths, destruction of infrastructure, political upheaval without end (see Afghanistan and Iraq), vast expense, and bitterness all around.

The Obama administration also seems determined to bring North Korea into line, by any means necessary. The US, which occupies countries all around poverty-stricken North Korea, is not only demonizing its alleged aggressiveness, it is making fun of its leader. It reminds me of the treatment of Saddam Hussein and other targeted enemies of the empire. But this whole business is more serious than that. Clearly the empire is targeting China, just as it did in Libya over oil. The US seeks to encircle China and make it bow down before the hegemon. The increasing prosperity and freedom of China threatens the empire's self image.

Readers might raise an objection here. Even if current foreign policy, under the guidance of the neocons, is as bad as we say it is, can the neocons' misdeeds be used to condemn American foreign policy altogether? Maybe the neocons are an aberration.

The historical record doesn't support this optimistic position. As Ron Paul has noted, "Neo-conservatism has been around for decades and, strangely, has connections to past generations as far back as Machiavelli. Modern-day neo-conservatism was introduced to us in the 1960s. It entails both a detailed strategy as well as a philosophy of government. The ideas of Teddy Roosevelt, and certainly Woodrow Wilson, were quite similar to many of the views of present-day neocons. Neocon spokesman Max Boot brags that what he advocates is "hard Wilsonianism." In many ways, there's nothing "neo" about their views, and certainly nothing conservative. Yet they have been able to co-opt the conservative movement by advertising themselves as a new or modern form of conservatism."

Following Ron Paul's lead, let's look at the first attempt to "make the world safe for democracy." When World War I broke out in Europe in August 1914, President Woodrow Wilson first called for Americans to be neutral in "thought as well as in action." But his heart wasn't in it. Britain, from the onset of war in 1914, had imposed a tight blockade on Germany; by preventing food from being imported into the country, the British brought starvation and malnutrition to large masses of the German people. As Senator Robert LaFollette pointed out, a food blockade violated international law and struck at America's rights as a neutral power. Even the British sometimes recognized the essential issue: According to Thomas Fleming in his excellent book *The Illusion of Victory*, "LaFollette cited an admission by Lord Salisbury, one of England's most prominent statesmen, that food for the civilian population was never contraband — a principle that the English were callously ignoring in their blockade of Germany."

German submarine warfare was a desperate response to the British starvation blockade — a blockade so effective that it threatened to force the Germans out of the war. But Wilson declined except in very restrained terms to challenge the British. In complete contrast, he held Germany to the strictest accountability.

But maybe Wilson's very unneutral "neutrality" was justifiable. British propaganda claimed that Germany was bent on world domination. If this was true, wasn't a victory of Britain and her allies in America's interest? But in fact the European War was no more than a power struggle. Contrary to Wilson and his Svengali-like adviser, Edward Mandell House, the First World War was not a struggle by the "democratic" countries, led by the British Empire, to stop autocratic Germany's bid for world control.

America, according to Wilson, had a mission to bring democracy to the world:

> It is a fearful thing to lead this great peaceful people into war, into the
> most terrible and disastrous of all wars, civilization itself seeming to
> hang in the balance. But the right is more precious than peace, and we

will fight for the things we have always carried in our hearts — for democracy ... for the rights and liberties of small nations, for a universal dominion of right by such a concert of free peoples as shall bring peace and safety to all nations and make the world at last free. ... America is privileged to spend her blood and her might for the principles that gave her birth and happiness and the peace which she has treasured. God helping her, she can do no other.

Wilson wasn't the only major force pressing America to enter World War I. The Morgan bank constantly aimed to subordinate the interests of the United States to British Empire. After the onset of World War I, "the Morgans played a substantial role in bringing the United States into the war on Britain's side, and, as head [i.e., most influential figure] of the Fed, Benjamin Strong obligingly doubled the money supply to finance America's role in the war effort."

Wilson, though extremely pro-British, began the process of replacing Britain with America as the dominant world power. Throughout the twentieth century, we see this constant pattern: America has used democratic rhetoric to impose American world domination. Let's look at one more example, the Cold War. (If we remember the Korean and Vietnam Wars, it wasn't so "cold.") The Cold War was sold to us as a battle against World Communism, which was hell-bent on overthrowing all non-Communist governments and subjecting the world to rule from Moscow. America, as always the champion of democracy, would save the world from the dire fate the Reds had in store for it.

Murray Rothbard pointed out the basic problem with this account. The "war" that the Communists waged against us was ideological. Though Communists might preach revolution, Soviet foreign policy posed no direct threat to America. Rothbard expressed this point in his customary trenchant way:

> But the Communists might stoop to violent revolution in America? Perhaps. But does anyone in his right mind believe that America faces the clear and present danger of overt, violent destruction by our tiny handful of domestic Communists?

> But the Communists have behind them a military base in the Soviet Union? Right, and that is why we should be happy that the Soviet Communists realize the futility of nuclear war, and call for peace. Khrushchev

and his successors have, frankly and honestly, been making their position unmistakably clear: they hope for internal adoption of communism in the U.S. and other countries, but they renounce any international, inter-state, *war*. This is what they mean by "peace," and this is what "peace" has always meant: absence of inter-state conflict. Why, then, must we simply assume that the men in the Kremlin are lying and that they don't want peace? Any rational person should prefer peace in the nuclear age. Let the ideological "war" with communism proceed, but let us also conclude military peace. Why, then, should we fear and hate the concept of "peaceful coexistence"? There is no basis on which to oppose it unless we think that freedom and free enterprise are ideologically *inferior* and could not survive an ideological debate with communism.

Why, then, did America wage the Cold War if it wasn't necessary to do so? We can find the answer in what is sometimes wrongly viewed as a protest against militarism, Eisenhower's farewell speech.

Eisenhower's farewell speech was a long and nearly hysterical argument for the Cold War. He presented it as more than a military policy against Russia, but rather as a grand metaphysical struggle that should take over our minds and souls, as bizarre as that must sound to the current generation.

His words were Wilsonian, even messianic. The job of US military policy is to "foster progress in human achievement" and enhance "dignity and integrity" the world over. That's a rather expansive role for government by any standard. But he went further. An enemy stands in the way of achieving this dream, and this enemy is "global in scope, atheistic in character, ruthless in purpose, and insidious in method." This great struggle "commands our whole attention, absorbs our very beings."

Because some crusty apparatchiks are imposing every manner of economic control over Russia and a few satellites, US foreign policy must absorb the whole of our beings? So much for limited government.

The rhetoric had to be hysterical to overcome a few obvious problems. Russia is a faraway country and the notion of an invasion was about as likely as one from Mars. Russia, an authoritarian state operating under the ideological cover of Communism, had only a few years earlier been declared our valiant ally in the struggle against Japan and Germany.

But Americans woke up one day to find that the line had suddenly changed: now Russia was the enemy to be defeated. In fact, the Russian government — already in deep economic trouble as a socialist regime — was bankrupted by World War II and dealing with incredible internal problems. The Soviets couldn't begin to manage the world of Eastern Europe that had been given as a prize for being the ally of the United States during the war. It was for this reason that Nikita Khrushchev began the first great period of liberalization that would end in the eventual unraveling of this nonviable state. The U.S. not only failed to encourage this liberalization, but pretended it wasn't happening so as to build up a new form of socialism at home.

Indeed, the entire Cold War ideology was invented by Harry Truman and his advisers in 1948 as: (1) a political trick to keep from losing more congressional backing, (2) a way to circumvent political pressure for postwar disarmament, and (3) a method to maintain US industrial dependence on government spending, particularly with regard to American corporations operating overseas.

It was an unprecedented form of peacetime socialism, designed to appeal to big business, and Eisenhower became its spokesman. Savvy libertarians knew exactly what was going on and supported Cold War opponent Robert Taft for the Republican nomination in 1952. But the nomination was effectively stolen by Eisenhower, with massive establishment backing. He repaid his backers with his support and expansion of Truman's program.

It's true that his farewell speech warned against "unwarranted influence, whether sought or unsought, by the military-industrial complex," and this is the part that people remember. But Eisenhower himself entrenched this very machinery in American life, virtually inventing the peacetime armaments industry and imposing military regimentation on the country. His approach was fundamentally un-American; or, another way to put it, he redefined what it meant to be an American. Instead of a free people, he forged a program for the permanent militarization of the country.

The evidence for this militarization begins with massive increases in military spending. As a percent of total budget outlays, military spending went from 30 percent in 1950 to 70 percent in 1957. This was the largest peacetime buildup in American history. During a dramatic economic expansion, the president worked to maintain a high military spending level as a percentage of the rising GDP — establishing the modern precedent that military socialism is integral to the economic life of the country. Spending rose in absolute terms every year he was president, from $358 billion in 1952 to $585 billion in the last budget for which he bore responsibility in 1962, a whopping 63.4 percent increase during the Eisenhower years.

His buildup was not limited to the arms sector; it penetrated every aspect of civilian life. Our schools were made to feature scary and abusive drills to practice what children should do if the Russians should drop bombs on their heads. An entire generation was raised with irrational fears of mythical threats.

Then there was the catastrophic Interstate Highway System, which was not built to make your trip to the beach go faster. Its purpose was to permit the military to move troops quickly. There were also cockamamie schemes of driving nuclear bombs around on those highways to prevent the commies from keeping track of them.

Eisenhower was influenced in funding this amazing boondoggle by his experience in 1919 with the Transcontinental Convoy on the Lincoln Highway, which drove military trucks from one coast to the other. Another influence was Hitler's project of building cross-country roads, again to move troops. The Interstate Highway System led to huge population upheavals and continues to distort commercial demographics in every town in the United States.

Given all this, the notion that Eisenhower was worried about the military-industrial complex is preposterous. He was devoted to it.

You might at this point raise a question. Even if American foreign policy since 1917 has been the ideologically-driven disaster portrayed here, why is this an argument for anarchism? Wouldn't it be enough if America abandoned its global crusade to promote democracy? After all, in the nineteenth century America followed the policy, set by Washington and Jefferson, of avoiding involvement in European power politics. If we returned to that policy today, wouldn't that be enough? Why do we need to get rid of the state entirely?

It's certainly true that Wilson and his successors broke with traditional American foreign policy. In his Farewell Address, George Washington said,

> Europe has a set of primary interests which to us have none; or a very remote relation. Hence she must be engaged in frequent controversies, the causes of which are essentially foreign to our concerns. Hence, therefore, it must be unwise of us to implicate ourselves by artificial ties in the ordinary vicissitudes of her politics, or the ordinary combinations and collisions of her friendships and enmities.

Thomas Jefferson confirmed and extended Washington's view of foreign affairs in his First Inaugural, supporting "peace, commerce, and friendship with all nations, entangling alliances with none."

The Monroe Doctrine reaffirmed this policy of non-intervention. In his message to Congress on Dec. 2, 1823, James Monroe stated:

> Our policy in regard to Europe, which was adopted at an early stage of the quarrels which have so agitated that quarter of the globe, nevertheless remains the same, which is, not to interfere in the internal concerns of any of its powers.

American foreign policy was indeed non-interventionist in the early years of the Republic, but only so far as Europe was concerned. Otherwise, America from the outset pursued an expansionist course. Oddly enough, one leading neocon, Robert Kagan, used this point in an effort to find historical precedents for neocon warmongering. In his book *Dangerous Nation*, Kagan gives a lengthy account of American expansion across the continent. In support of the constant hunger of Americans for land, he shows, the United States government was often quite willing to challenge the powers of Europe forcibly. He complains that diplomatic historians have wrongly separated this saga of expansion from their accounts of foreign policy. These historians classify expansion across the American continent as a domestic affair, and by doing so they can claim that American foreign policy was isolationist. But they pass over the fact that the domestic expansion involved conflicts with foreign powers. If they took account of this, they would have to abandon their thesis of American isolation.

Although Kagan wrongly projects recent efforts to make the world safe for democracy onto America's past, he is right that America has always grabbed territory, often at the expense of the lives and property rights of Indians. To say, "we need to return to the foreign policy of the Founders" won't solve our problem. Even if we did this, we would still be violating the just war principles that Rothbard has set out. And let's not forget the War of 1812, in part motivated by the wish to conquer Canada, and the Mexican War, aptly called in a recent book *A Wicked War*.

This book isn't a history of American foreign policy, but we can't pass by with just a mention the greatest of all nineteenth-century violations of just war principles; the War Between the States. It is clear that Lincoln's decision to use force against the Southern states that had seceded did not meet the just war criteria. States under the Constitution had the legal right to secede. As Kevin Gutzman points out in *The Politically Incorrect Guide to the Constitution*, to understand the meaning of the Constitution we need to look at the intentions of the delegates to the ratifying conventions. These delegates, after all, were the people whose votes established the Constitution as legally binding. Gutzman concentrates on the Virginia convention, and he places great stress on one point.

The Virginia delegates looked on the new Constitution with great skepticism, fearing that it would become a tool for the federal government to crush the states. To placate opponents such as Patrick Henry, the leaders of the pro-ratification forces, who included Governor Edmund Randolph, the proposer of the nationalist Virginia Plan at Philadelphia, had to make a concession. They had to agree that the powers of the new Congress were limited to those "expressly delegated" in the Constitution. The delegates repudiated in advance any move by the new authorities to expand their powers beyond this. Further, they wrote into their ratification statement the right to withdraw from the new government, if it exceeded its proper powers.

Gutzman contends that because this understanding was part of Virginia's instrument of ratification, no stronger central government can claim Virginia's authorization. And since it would be senseless to think that the Constitution gives the federal government more power over some states than others, the Virginia restrictions apply to all the states.

This is the Jeffersonian view of the Constitution. Gutzman's great contribution is to show that the Virginia and Kentucky Resolutions of 1798 and 1799, the key statements of the Jeffersonian position, restated the understanding of the Virginia ratifying convention. Contrary to the Federalist opponents of the Resolutions, Jefferson and Madison did not act as innovators in 1798; and their position cannot be dismissed as merely one of several competing interpretations. It was firmly based on the legally valid Virginia ratification instrument.

Gutzman summarizes his main contention in this way:

> Most history and legal textbooks say that Jefferson and Madison invented the idea of state sovereignty. But ... they only argued for what the founders had already understood to be true about the sovereign states from the beginning, even if some of the founders (the nationalist and monarchist wings) wanted to change that understanding.

What was the reason for Lincoln's policy? It was not, as popular mythology has it, to end slavery. Lincoln was ready to support a Constitutional Amendment that guaranteed to preserve slavery. Thomas DiLorenzo points out in *Lincoln Unmasked* that Lincoln referred to the proposal, the Corwin Amendment, in his First Inaugural, stating that he was not opposed to the amendment, since it merely made explicit the existing constitutional arrangement regarding slavery. Of course, Lincoln was here characteristically lying; nothing in the Constitution before this amendment prohibited amendments to end slavery.

So much is well established, but DiLorenzo adds a surprising touch. Far from viewing the Corwin Amendment with grudging consent, Lincoln was in fact its behind-the-scenes promoter.

> As soon as he was elected, but before his inauguration, Lincoln "instructed [Secretary of State] Seward to introduce [the amendment] in the Senate Committee of Thirteen without indicating they issued from Springfield." ... In addition, Lincoln instructed Seward to get through Congress a law that would make the various "personal liberty laws" that existed in some Northern states illegal. (Such state laws nullified the Federal Fugitive Slave Act, which required Northerners to apprehend runaway slaves.)

The key to Lincoln's policy toward the states that had seceded may be found in a passage of his First Inaugural, delivered on March 4, 1861. Here he said that he would not initiate force against the departed states, even though in his view they had acted illegally in seceding. His seemingly conciliatory policy was belied by a qualification. He said that he would not use force, except to the extent necessary to collect the duties and imposts.

In his First Inaugural, Lincoln said:

> The power confided in me [Lincoln] will be used to hold, occupy, and possess the property and places belonging to the government, and to collect the duties and imposts; but beyond what may be necessary for these objects, there will be no invasion, no using of force against or among the people anywhere.

The government of the United States depended at that time for its revenue principally on tariffs. These operated to the disadvantage of the South, a largely agricultural area, which had to pay high prices for imports. Tariffs redistributed wealth from the South to the North.

Another development which began to divide the North and South was that the political power of the North allowed it to keep a vast majority of the tariff revenue and use it for "internal improvements," such as building harbors and canals, which was, in effect, a corporate welfare program.

Northern interests added to Southern misery by using the tariff explicitly for industrial protection, culminating in the Morrill Tariff, passed by the Senate in February 1861, after a number of states had already seceded, and avidly promoted by Lincoln. By seceding, the South threatened this entire system. By instituting a free-trade zone — or at least by drastically undercutting Northern tariffs — the South could divert the bulk of international trade to Southern ports; Northern business would be struck a severe blow and the federal government would be compelled to seek an alternative system of revenue. Lincoln, a firm believer in tariffs, was determined to prevent this from happening. Thus he insisted that the duties and imposts would be collected.

As the great nineteenth-century abolitionist and libertarian Lysander Spooner pointed out, the primary motive of Lincoln and the war party was to preserve and consolidate Northern control of the Southern economy. The Southern states could not be allowed to evade the tariff, a key element of the mercantilist American system that Lincoln favored.

Spooner wrote that the war "erupted for a purely pecuniary consideration," and not for any moral reason. He labeled the economic lifeblood of the Republican Party, Northern bankers, manufacturers, and railroad corporations, "lenders of blood money." ... To Spooner the Northern financiers of the war who had lent money to the Lincoln government did so not for "any love of liberty or justice," but for the control of [Southern] markets' through "tariff extortion." ... Spooner interpreted the crushing of the Southern secessionists ... as suggesting that Southerners should "Submit quietly to all the robbery and slavery we have arranged for you, and you can have your peace."

America has never adhered to the strict requirements of the just war tradition; but we need now to answer an important question. Why does the government keep acting in this unjust way? Wars are after all destructive; why then engage in them?

In his great book *Crisis and Leviathan*, Robert Higgs has supplied an important part of the answer. The state grows during wartime and other "emergencies"; and when peace or normality returns, government does not shrink to its former size. Business groups that might have been expected to defend free enterprise in fact cooperate with the government in order to advance their own interests. Higgs notes:

Within three decades, from the outbreak of World War I in Europe to the end of World War II, the American people endured three great national emergencies, during each of which the federal government imposed unprecedented taxation and economic controls on the population. ... Rather than resisting the government's impositions or working to over- throw them, they [business interests] looked for ways to adapt to them, positioning themselves so that the government policies would provide a tax advantage, channel a subsidy their way, or hobble their competitors.

The policy that Charles Beard called "perpetual war for perpetual peace" serves the ends of the elite who increase their own power and wealth through making the State larger.

Before we turn from the State and its war system, we need to confront one more objection. We have claimed that the American State has constantly involved us in unjust wars. Not even going back to non-intervention will solve the problem: the State systematically grows in power and can't be contained, so long as it remains a State. But, the objection goes, aren't some wars just? How could we reasonably have stayed out of World War II? Only a large-scale State could wage war against Nazi Germany. Without powerful governments, the world would have been at the mercy of Hitler.

Rothbard of course was well aware of this objection. He followed A.J.P Taylor in thinking that Hitler had not planned a world war. Instead, the war came about as the result of a series of diplomatic blunders. More, generally, he said:

> It is about time that Americans learn: that Bad Guys (Nazis or Communists) may not necessarily want or desire war, or be out to "conquer" the world (their hope for "conquest" may be strictly ideological and not military at all); that Bad Guys may also fear the possibility of our use of our enormous military might and aggressive posture to attack them; that both the Bad Guys and Good Guys may have common interests which make negotiation possible (e.g., that neither wants to be annihilated by nuclear weapons); that no organization is a "monolith," and that "agents" are often simply ideological allies who can and do split with their supposed "masters"; and that, finally, we may learn the most profound lesson of all: that the domestic policy of a government is often no index whatever to its foreign policy.

> We are still, in the last analysis, suffering from the delusion of Woodrow Wilson: that "democracies" *ipso facto* will never embark on war, and that "dictatorships" are always prone to engage in war. Much as we may and do abhor the domestic programs of most dictators (and certainly of the Nazis and Communists), this has no necessary relation to their foreign policies: indeed, many dictatorships have been passive and static in history, and, contrariwise, many democracies have led in promoting and waging war. Revisionism may, once and for all, be able to destroy this Wilsonian myth.

But what if Rothbard was wrong? What if the Nazis *did* aim at world conquest? There was still no valid reason for America to enter World War II before the Pearl Harbor attack. If this is right, the objection to our case against the war system fails. The great libertarian Garet Garrett illustrates our point. He thought that the Nazis posed a threat to us, but that we should respond with a policy of watchful waiting.

In an editorial for the *Saturday Evening Post* of July 6, 1940, Garrett said:

A new and frightful power has appeared, an offensive power moved by an unappeasable earth hunger, conscious of no right but the right of might. It does not threaten this country with invasion: at least, not yet. It does threaten the Western Hemisphere by economic and political designs in the Latin American countries, and this is, for us, an ominous fact. But the larger aspect of what has happened is that the world is in a state of unbalance.

Garrett's decisive move was to deny that an adequate response to Hitler required military aid to the Allies. Just the opposite, America should make its borders secure from attack:

In the whole world ... there is one people able to create a defensive power equal to the new power of frightful aggression that has destroyed the basis of international peace and civility. We are that people ... we are the most nearly self-contained nation of modern times, an empire entire, possessing of our own in plenty practically every essential thing. ... Our productive power is equal to that of all Europe, and may be increased, so far as we know, without limit. ... Finally, as we lie between two oceans, our geographical advantages in the military sense are such as to give us great natural odds against any aggressor.

Defenders of American intervention in the war might answer Garrett in this way: "Maybe America can do as you say. But why should we retreat to a Fortress America? If, as you concede, Germany menaces us, why should we not aid those already struggling against the Third Reich and its Führer?"

Garrett fully anticipated this objection, and in his response he showed himself a better economist than his critics. If America sent arms to other countries, wouldn't this weaken our own forces? Interventionists thought only of the benefits that aid would help secure, but they ignored the fact that stripping America of its arms weakened us, especially so because America had not yet built up secure defenses. In sum, Garrett, unlike his critics, was fully alive to the concept of opportunity cost.

If it should turn out that to strip this country of armaments and send them to Europe at a moment when our existing power of defense was pitifully inadequate ... had been a tragic blunder ... then the leader who had done it might wish that his page in the book of fame might refuse to receive ink, for it would be written of him that in his passionate zeal to save civilization in Europe he had forgotten his own country.

But we must overcome a final objection. What about Pearl Harbor? Didn't the Japanese attack us? If so, weren't we engaged after this in a just war of defense? These questions depend on a naïve view of the facts. As the distinguished UCLA diplomatic historian and political scientist Marc Trachtenberg has pointed out, Roosevelt wanted to enter the war in Europe. But how was he to do so? Hitler, knowing that the American president viewed him as an enemy, carefully avoided clashes with American ships, despite an aggressive American naval policy directed against Germany.

For this reason, Trachtenberg thinks, Roosevelt looked to Japan. He imposed an embargo on oil exports, posing a mortal threat to the Japanese economy. Wasn't this a provocative move designed to induce the desperate Japanese to attack the United States?

How, though, would a Japanese attack involve us in war with Germany? Many historians have seen in this question a decisive objection to the "back door to war" thesis. Trachtenberg has a brilliant response to this powerful objection. It rests, he holds, on a false assumption. Once America and Japan were at war, why would the decision for war with Germany rest only with Hitler? Wouldn't Roosevelt have then been able to overcome isolationist resistance and secure from Congress a declaration of war against Germany?

> The Axis alliance ... came to be seen as much tighter than it actually was. And it was in large part for that reason that Pearl Harbor was widely blamed on the Axis as a whole. Indeed, many people throughout the country ... were convinced at the time of the Pearl Harbor attack that the Japanese were "Hitler's puppets." And Roosevelt, of course, would not have been unaware of something this basic. ... He might well have reached the conclusion that Germany would not be able to stay out of a U.S.-Japanese war, no matter what decision Hitler made. And what this means is that a back-door strategy, if that is what it was, might well have been workable in that political context.

Trachtenberg's argument receives further support from the fact that following the attack on Pearl Harbor, not even the America First Committee thought that there was a realistic chance of separating war with

Japan and war with Germany. It mounted no campaign to confine the war to Asia, and the Committee disbanded on December 11, the day that Germany declared war on the United States.

We can go further. As usual, Robert Higgs gets at the essence of things:

> Because American cryptographers had also broken the Japanese naval code, the leaders in Washington also knew that Japan's "measures" would include an attack on Pearl Harbor. Yet they withheld this critical information from the commanders in Hawaii, who might have headed off the attack or prepared themselves to defend against it. That Roosevelt and his chieftains did not ring the tocsin makes perfect sense: after all, the impending attack constituted precisely what they had been seeking for a long time. As Stimson confided to his diary after a meeting of the War Cabinet on November 25, "The question was how we should maneuver them [the Japanese] into firing the first shot without allowing too much danger to ourselves." After the attack, Stimson confessed that "my first feeling was of relief ... that a crisis had come in a way which would unite all our people."

In his efforts to involve the United States in war with the Axis, Roosevelt had the aid of British intelligence. Thomas Mahl, in his important book *Desperate Deception*, has greatly clarified the scope and nature of British activities designed to involve America in war: The single most striking example of the effectiveness of the British effort is this. Before the Office of Strategic Services (OSS) was established, a presidential directive in July 1941 set up a preliminary group called The Coordinator of Information (COI). Not only was this group, which devised the plans for the OSS, organized because British Intelligence had asked for it; its head was a British agent. Colonel Charles Howard "Dick" Ellis, an assistant to the principal British intelligence agent in America, Sir William Stephenson, "actually ran [William] Donovan's COI office and produced the blueprint for the American OSS."

I won't describe in detail the vast range of episodes which Mahl discusses. Rather let's look at two additional examples of British influence. The first relates to the crucial US election of November 1940. In order to win the war, Britain needed the support of the United States as a fighting ally. But, if the Republicans ran a strong non-interventionist campaign, not even the tricks of Franklin Roosevelt would be able to get America into the war. "The first peacetime draft law in American history, Burke-

Wadsworth, and the Destroyer Deal would not have received Roosevelt's endorsement had a genuine opposition candidate stood ready to make it a political issue in the 1940 election."

To secure the British goal, then, the Republican candidate had to be solidly in the interventionist camp. How could this be achieved? Mahl answers his question by pointing to something very unexpected at the time: the unexpected surge of support for Wendell Willkie in the months before the Republican convention, and at the convention itself.

The stampede toward Willkie, the quintessential dark horse candidate, puzzled informed contemporaries. H.L. Mencken "wrote, after watching the nomination: 'I am thoroughly convinced that the nomination of Willkie was managed by the Holy Ghost in person.'" Mahl has a more down-to-earth explanation. The boom for Willkie was plotted with heavy British support; the banker Thomas W. Lamont played a key role in the effort.

In any event, once nominated Willkie enabled the British strategy to carry on without fundamental challenge from the Republican candidate. Mahl cites in this connection a telling remark of Walter Lippmann, himself an ally of British intelligence: "Second only to the Battle of Britain, the sudden rise and nomination of Wendell Willkie was the decisive event, perhaps providential, which made it possible to rally the free world when it was almost conquered." Willkie was if anything more interventionist than Roosevelt; non-interventionist voters in 1940 were in effect shut out of the presidential election.

Another key issue also involves the paralysis of isolationist opposition to British plans. Senator Arthur Vandenberg of Michigan, a protégé of the isolationist William Borah, ranked among the foremost non-interventionists during the 1930s. He executed a sudden reversal in July 1940 and supported the crucial Lend-Lease Bill in March 1941.

Mahl attributes the change of heart to the influence of Mitzi Sims, Vandenberg's mistress, who had strong ties to British intelligence, and of another woman, Betty Thorpe Pack ("Cynthia"), also romantically linked with him. Mahl admits he cannot prove that Vandenberg's relationship with those women changed the senator's views; but his conjecture certainly helps us understand Vandenberg's otherwise inexplicable behavior.

Throughout American history, we have shown, America did not follow the rules of the just war tradition in getting involved in war. But, as Rothbard explained, the just war rules did not stop there. Besides the limits on when war is justified, Rothbard also emphasized restrictions on the conduct of war. In his essay "Just War" in *Secession, State, and Liberty*, he says:

> Specifically, the classical international lawyers developed two ideas, which they were broadly successful in getting nations to adopt: (1) above all, don't target civilians. If you must fight, let the rulers and their loyal or hired retainers slug it out, but keep civilians on both sides out of it, as much as possible. The growth of democracy, the identification of citizens with the State, conscription, and the idea of a "nation in arms," all whittled away this excellent tenet of international law.

> (2) Preserve the rights of neutral states and nations. In the modern corruption of international law that has prevailed since 1914, "neutrality" has been treated as somehow deeply immoral. Nowadays, if countries A and B get into a fight, it becomes every nation's moral obligation to figure out, quickly, which country is the "bad guy," and then if, say, A is condemned as the bad guy, to rush in and pummel A in defense of the alleged good guy B.

Classical international law, which should be brought back as quickly as possible, was virtually the opposite. In a theory which tried to limit war, neutrality was considered not only justifiable but a positive virtue. In the old days, "he kept us out of war" was high tribute to a president or political leader; but now, all the pundits and professors condemn any president who "stands idly by" while "people are being killed" in Bosnia, Somalia, Rwanda, or the hot spot of the day. In the old days, "standing idly by" was considered a mark of high statesmanship. Not only that: neutral states had "rights" which were mainly upheld, since every warring country knew that someday it too would be neutral. A warring state could not interfere with neutral shipping to an enemy state; neutrals could ship to such an enemy with impunity all goods except "contraband," which was strictly defined as arms and ammunition, period. Wars were kept limited in those days, and neutrality was extolled.

Judged by these standards, American policy also falls short. Let's look at just two examples, both unfortunately horrendous. General Sherman deliberately targeted civilians during the War Between the States. He continued this policy in campaigns after the war against the Indians, often with genocidal results. Tom DiLorenzo points out that Sherman said the following about the Plains Indians shortly after the war:

> "It is one of those irreconcilable conflicts that will end only in one way, one or the other must be exterminated. ... We must act with vindictive earnestness against the Sioux, even to their extermination, men, women and children." Sherman had given [General Phillip] Sheridan prior authorization to slaughter as many women and children as well as men Sheridan or his subordinates felt was necessary. ... Sherman would cover the political and media front and maintained personal deniability. "The more Indians we can kill this year, the less will have to be killed next year," wrote Sherman. "They all have to be killed or be maintained as a species of paupers."

> Sherman said this about Southerners:

> To the petulant and persistent secessionists, why death is mercy, and the quicker he or *she* is disposed of the better. ... Until we can repopulate Georgia, it is useless to occupy it, but the utter destruction of its roads, houses, *and people* will cripple their military resources. (emphasis added)

> Here you have a clear statement that Sherman's goal was to commit genocide against the people of Georgia. Remember that his famous "march" was not met by any serious military resistance other than a few cavalry skirmishes. It was almost entirely a campaign of death and destruction of civilians and their property. And he wanted to "repopulate" the state with fine New England stock such as himself, the son of a New England lawyer of Puritan descent."

Atrocities against civilians continued in the twentieth century. During World War II, the United States directly targeted civilians though massive terror bombing. The atomic destruction of Hiroshima and Nagasaki is of course the most notorious example of this; amazingly, some supporters of the State's war system still defend it. They say that the atomic assault saved lives. Without the bombing, America would have launched a massive invasion of Japan that would have cost even more lives than those lost in the bombing.

This argument doesn't work. Even if atomic bombs cost fewer lives than an invasion would have done, why are bombing and an invasion the only alternatives? Why did we have to conquer Japan at all? In 1945, Japan no longer posed a threat to us. We should have been willing to negotiate a settlement with the Japanese, instead of insisting on unconditional surrender.

In 1956, Oxford University was going to grant an honorary degree to ex-President Truman. Elizabeth Anscombe, who was a famous Oxford philosopher and taught at Somerville College, was outraged. She wrote a pamphlet, "Mr. Truman's Degree," that protested against the award. She attracted a lot of notice in the newspapers, but the Oxford faculty voted to go ahead with the degree.

She lost the vote, but her argument against Truman's policy was a good one. She wrote:

> I do not dispute it. Given the conditions, that [an invasion costly in lives] was probably averted by that action. But what were the conditions? The unlimited objective. Given certain conditions, drastic measures appear needed; but should this very fact not make us take a close look at the supposed necessities of the present state of things? If we do not, but instead insist that extreme circumstances demand extreme responses, we are in danger of adopting the maxim that "every fool can be as much of a knave as suits him."

In other words, you can't justify an atrocity by claiming that without it, a goal of yours would require even more costly measures. Instead, you should abandon the goal. Of course those leaders of the warfare state were unwilling to do this.

2

THE WAR ON DRUGS

THE AMERICAN GOVERNMENT, THUS, has continually violated the laws of war. The aggressive wars that the American state has waged, though, have not been confined to wars against other states. As we'll see again and again in this book, the American state wages war against our own people, the people it is supposed to protect and defend. In this chapter, we will see one way that it does this. A draconian policy of drug regulation needlessly puts thousands of people in jail and discriminates against blacks, for a completely illegitimate purpose. Drugs, it is claimed harm those who take them. Even if this claim is true, why should you be put in jail for harming yourself? It makes no sense. Douglas Husak, a legal philosopher who teaches at Rutgers, asks,

> Does anyone believe that individuals should be punished for something simply because the failure to do so would cause an increase in the behavior for which they are punished? This rationale fails to provide the personal justification for punishment that is needed. This is not our reason to criminalize acts like murder and rape. No one would say that we should punish such acts simply because the failure to do so might lead others to commit rape and murder.

To punish people simply because their acts encourage others to act in a way deemed undesirable is to use people as a mere means to an end, in a morally unacceptable way. If the state can imprison someone because his drug use sets a bad example to children, or helps to maintain a market in drugs associated with violent crime, isn't the state failing to treat the drug user as a human being worthy of respect?

Why should people be prevented from selling consumers what they want to buy? Those who run afoul of the law by peddling drugs often get unbelievably harsh prison sentences — for something that in a free society shouldn't be a crime at all. As if this were not bad enough, making drugs illegal promotes real crimes and violence.

There is one simple argument that shows immediately that the underlying basis of the war on drugs collapses. Almost everybody today realizes that Prohibition was a failure: the attempt to regulate alcohol consumption didn't work and brought crime and civil liberties violations in its wake. People now realize that the harms that result from alcohol abuse don't justify the restrictions on liberty that the prohibitionists imposed. The evidence that abuse of alcohol blights certain lives is far stronger than conjectures that some have about the abuse of heroin by poor and untalented teenagers. But if most people reject the Prohibition Amendment as an undue restriction on personal freedom, shouldn't they reject the war on drugs as well? As Laurence Vance points out,

> Alcohol abuse and heavy tobacco use are two of the leading causes of death in the United States. It seems rather ludicrous to advocate the outlawing of drugs and not the outlawing of alcohol and tobacco.

The drug laws have had life-shattering consequences for many people. Again Laurence Vance states the essential facts in clear and cogent fashion:

> The United States leads the world in the incarceration rate and in the total prison population. ... Almost twenty percent of the state prison population are incarcerated because of drug charges. Almost half of the federal prison population are incarcerated because of drug charges. There are almost 350,000 Americans in state or federal prison at this moment [November 2011] because of drug charges.

You might think, "This may be bad, but it doesn't really affect me — I don't use drugs." But matters are not so simple.

> The war on drugs has destroyed financial privacy. Deposit more than $10,000 in a bank account and you are a suspected drug trafficker. ... The war on drugs has provided the rationale for militarizing local

police departments. ... The war on drugs has resulted in outrageous behavior by police in their quest to arrest drug dealers. ... The war on drugs has eviscerated the Fourth Amendment's prohibition against unreasonable searches and seizures.

Further, once the government gets its foot in the door in regulating your personal behavior, there is no logical stopping point. If the government can control what goes into your body why can't it control what goes into your mind as well? As Ludwig von Mises pointed out,

Opium and morphine are certainly dangerous, habit-forming drugs. But once the principle is admitted that it is the duty of the government to protect the individual against his own foolishness, no serious objections can be advanced against further encroachments. ... And why limit the government's benevolent providence to the protection of the individual's body only? Is not the harm a man can inflict on his mind and soul even more disastrous than any bodily evils? Why not prevent him from reading bad books and seeing bad plays, from looking at bad paintings and statues and from hearing bad music?

The Drug War violates everybody's liberty, but it hurts one minority group particularly hard: American blacks. Wilt Alston gives us the grim facts:

How can one say the drug war is racist? Let us start with some pretty basic numbers: Black people — men, women, and children — compose approximately 12.6 percent of the population of the United States. Black people — primarily black men — compose approximately 35.4% of the prison population. Anyone not living under a large stone or just arriving to Earth from another galaxy already knows America has a *very* healthy prison population ... the bottom line is this. The U.S. incarceration rate is over 700 people per 100,000 of population. The next highest rate is either in New Zealand at approximately 168 per 100,000 or Spain at approximately 164 per 100,000, dependent upon who is counting and which chart one examines.

So putting folks in jail is a hobby for the American State. Putting black folks in prison, well, that's just a bonus! "Amerika" has more people in prison than any other nation on Earth, and the percentage of those people who are black and male is roughly three times the percentage of black people in the general population. Why? ... [One suggestion] is because black people commit more drug crimes, and, therefore, get arrested more, convicted more, and incarcerated more. Each of these statements is so ignorant as to be comical, but more importantly, each of them is so cataclysmically incorrect as to be criminal, pardon the pun.

First of all, with the possible exception of crack cocaine, black people do not abuse drugs at a higher level than white people; that is, the absolute number of drug users who are black is lower. Ergo, the assertion is incorrect on its face, as evidenced by a study published in *The Stanford Law and Policy Review*.

Here's the thing, though. It is possible (nay, even likely) that black men *do* get arrested more, convicted more, and incarcerated more. That does not mean that they, in fact, commit more drug-related crime. The available data illustrate rather starkly that for illicit drug use, black people are not leading the parade. (Let us, for the time being, put aside the issue of whether or not any person putting a substance into his own body can *ever* truly be criminal for the moment, since the overwhelming majority of Americans may actually believe that the State *establishes* what is criminal versus *discovers* it.)

Secondly, the mathematics of drug distribution and drug production preclude the possibility that a group so small as black males could possibly be responsible at a level to justify their incarceration rate. In other words, drugs like crack and weed are produced in large quantities, but could be manufactured and packaged pretty much anywhere, assuming the raw materials are present. However, the sheer amount that is being produced and distributed suggests a larger operation than could be supported by just black folks. For more "sophisticated" drugs like heroin and cocaine, it seems that the production is almost exclusively off-shore. The finished product is then shipped into the States. Do you reckon there are lots of boats and planes berthed in the Inner City, where the predominant arrests of black males are made? Of course not. Yet, drug warriors continue to target and arrest black men, and ignorant people continue to deny that there is a racial component afoot. Notes [Charles] Blow:

> … no group has been more targeted and suffered more damage than the black community. As the A.C.L.U. pointed out. … "The racial disparities [in drug arrests and prosecution] are staggering: despite the fact that whites engage in drug offenses at a higher rate than African-Americans, African-Americans are incarcerated at a rate that is ten times greater than that of whites."

Black people, comprising 12.6 percent of the U.S. population —
are incarcerated for drug offences at a rate 10 times higher than
that of whites — resulting in 35.4 percent of the overall prison
population. If that doesn't sound like an old-school racist's wet
dream, I don't know what does. (Sure, *all* the black folks in prison
aren't there for drug offenses, but the overwhelming majority of
people in prison are there for non-violent drug offenses.)

There's a closely related area to the war on drugs in which the State
has assaulted our rights — laws that forbid drunk driving. Now the feds
declare that a blood-alcohol level of 0.08 percent and above is criminal
and must be severely punished. The National Restaurant Association
is exactly right that this is absurdly low. The overwhelming majority of
accidents related to drunk driving involve repeat offenders with blood-
alcohol levels twice that high. If a standard of 0.1 doesn't deter them,
then a lower one won't either.

But there's a more fundamental point. What precisely is being criminalized? Not bad driving. Not destruction of property. Not the taking
of human life or reckless endangerment. The crime is having the wrong
substance in your blood. Yet it is possible, in fact, to have this substance
in your blood, even while driving, and not commit anything like what
has been traditionally called a crime.

What have we done by permitting government to criminalize the
content of our blood instead of actions themselves? We have given it
power to make the application of the law arbitrary, capricious, and contingent on the judgment of cops and cop technicians. Indeed, without
the government's "Breathalyzer," there is no way to tell for sure if we are
breaking the law.

Sure, we can do informal calculations in our head, based on our
weight and the amount of alcohol we have had over some period of time.
But at best these will be estimates. We have to wait for the government to
administer a test to tell us whether or not we are criminals. That's not the
way law is supposed to work. Indeed, this is a form of tyranny.

Now, the immediate response goes this way: drunk driving has to be
illegal because the probability of causing an accident rises dramatically
when you drink. The answer is just as simple: government in a free society should not deal in probabilities. The law should deal in actions and

actions alone, and only insofar as they damage person or property. Probabilities are something for insurance companies to assess on a competitive and voluntary basis.

This is why the campaign against "racial profiling" has intuitive plausibility to many people: surely a person shouldn't be hounded solely because some demographic groups have higher crime rates than others. Government should be preventing and punishing crimes themselves, not probabilities and propensities. Neither, then, should we have driver profiling, which assumes that just because a person has quaffed a few he is automatically a danger.

In fact, driver profiling is worse than racial profiling, because the latter only implies that the police are more watchful, not that they criminalize race itself. Despite the propaganda, what's being criminalized in the case of drunk driving is *not* the probability that a person driving will get into an accident but the *fact* of the blood-alcohol content itself. A drunk driver is humiliated and destroyed even when he hasn't done any harm.

Of course, enforcement is a serious problem. A sizeable number of people leaving a bar or a restaurant would probably qualify as DUI. But there is no way for the police to know unless they are tipped off by a swerving car or reckless driving in general. But the question becomes: why not ticket the swerving or recklessness and leave the alcohol out of it? Why indeed.

To underscore the fact that it is some level of drinking that is being criminalized, government sets up these outrageous, civil-liberties-violating barricades that stop people to check their blood — even when they have done nothing at all. This is a gross attack on liberty that implies that the government has and should have total control over us, extending even to the testing of intimate biological facts. But somehow we put up with it because we have conceded the first assumption that government ought to punish us for the content of our blood and not just our actions.

There are many factors that cause a person to drive poorly. You may have sore muscles after a weight-lifting session and have slow reactions. You could be sleepy. You could be in a bad mood, or angry after a fight with your spouse. Should the government be allowed to administer anger tests, tiredness tests, or soreness tests? That is the very next step, and don't be surprised when Congress starts to examine this question.

Already, there's a move on to prohibit cell phone use while driving. Such an absurdity follows from the idea that government should make judgments about what we are allegedly likely to do.

What's more, some people drive *more* safely after a few drinks, precisely because they know their reaction time has been slowed and they must pay more attention to safety. We all know drunks who have an amazing ability to drive perfectly after being liquored up. They should be liberated from the force of the law, and only punished if they actually do something wrong.

We need to put a stop to this whole trend now. Drunk driving should be legalized. And please don't write me to say: "I am offended by your insensitivity because my mother was killed by a drunk driver." Any person responsible for killing someone else is guilty of manslaughter or murder and should be punished accordingly. But it is perverse to punish a murderer not because of his crime but because of some biological consideration, e.g., he has red hair.

Bank robbers may tend to wear masks, but the crime they commit has nothing to do with the mask. In the same way, drunk drivers cause accidents but so do sober drivers, and many drunk drivers cause no accidents at all. The law should focus on violations of person and property, not scientific oddities like blood content.

There's still another way that the State's involvement in drugs affects nearly everybody. The State controls what medical drugs we can use. In order for a new drug to gain government approval, it must pass stringent regulations devised by the Federal Drug Administration. These regulations have kept off the market drugs that could have saved many lives. But you can suppose a proponent of regulation says, "True enough, the FDA has delayed some valuable drugs. But it has kept dangerous drugs from harming people. When you condemn the FDA, you show only that you and that agency weigh costs and benefits differently."

As the great historian Robert Higgs has emphasized, this reply doesn't work. The FDA's attempt to give us "safe" drugs has been a miserable failure. "According to one study, "fatal reactions to FDA-approved drugs amount to the fourth-leading cause of death in the United States, after heart disease, cancer, and stroke." And to those still reluctant to abandon the comforting myth that the FDA protects us from harm, Higgs has at the ready another surprising fact: "Once a drug has been approved, doctors are not restricted to using it solely for the FDA-approved indication; they may prescribe it for other uses as well. Such uses, known as 'off-label,' account for some 40–50 percent of all prescriptions." The costs of drug regulation are real, the benefits illusory.

If the State can tell us what drugs we can take, there is a logical next step. Every society must answer a fundamental question about its medical system. Does each person control his own body? If he does, he has the right to decide what type of medical treatment he wants. If people do not own their own bodies, then medical policy need not respect individual decisions, and individuals can be ruthlessly cast aside for the supposed general welfare.

There is no doubt about how the Nazis answered our question. Paul Diepgen, the leading historian of medicine in the Third Reich and also during the preceding Weimar Republic, said in a book that appeared in 1938: "National Socialism means something fundamentally new for medical life. It has overcome an idea that was central to medicine of the recent past: the idea of the right to one's own body." A key Nazi slogan was "The common good is higher than the individual good."

If individuals do not make the key medical decisions, who does? Inevitably, it is those who control the state. The Nazis denied that they subordinated everything to the state; in contrast to Italian fascism, their propaganda stressed the party rather than the state. But in practice, this did not matter. To them, the welfare of the German people, the *Deutsche Volk*, was the supreme good; and Hitler, as the Leader of the German people, claimed the right to be the final judge of what best promoted this. In his Berlin Sportpalast speech of January 30, 1941, he declared that he had a democratic mandate and had come to power legally. His will, and the decisions of his chosen subordinates, thus determined medical policy, as it did everything else of significance.

If individuals do not own their own bodies, then people have no right to reproduce. The good of the German *Volk*, as determined by the ruling authorities, would govern who could have children. A law of October

1933 provided for the sterilization of persons with certain conditions, including feeblemindedness, schizophrenia, manic-depression, epilepsy, blindness, deafness, and alcoholism. Genetic courts could judge people with these conditions. These consisted of two doctors and a lawyer. Eminent scientists, including Eugen Fischer, who coined the word "genetics" in 1926, served on the tribunals. People could appeal the verdict of the genetics court, but few appeals were successful. About 4,000 people per year were sterilized, mostly for feeblemindedness; the total number of people sterilized under this law was about 400,000. Rudolf Ramm, a leading National Socialist medical expert, said that those sterilized were making a sacrifice "in the interests of the good of the *Volk*."

Here I think we must avoid a mistake. It is easy to say that such a policy could only take place in a dictatorship: a Western democracy could never do such a thing. Quite the contrary, sterilization was very popular in the United States. Twenty-nine states had laws allowing compulsory sterilization, beginning with Indiana in 1907. Oliver Wendell Holmes found these laws constitutional in *Buck v. Bell* (1927). He declared, "three generations of imbeciles are enough." In fact, the Nazis modeled their policy on the American laws. They were influenced by American racial theorists and eugenicists, such as Lothrop Stoddard. He later visited Germany and described the genetic courts in his book *Into the Darkness.* European nations such as Denmark also had sterilization laws. Once a nation abandons self-ownership, individual welfare must indeed bow to the general good. The National Socialists carried out more consistently than others an idea that was widespread.

3

THE ASSAULT ON OUR LIBERTIES

WE'VE ALREADY SEEN SEVERAL areas in which the State is making war on us. Unfortunately, there are many others — we can't get away from them. In this chapter, we'll look at a few more.

One of the main ways our freedom has been taken away stems from a movement explicitly hostile to people. No, this is not a misprint — a very powerful ideology explicitly hates human beings and looks forward to wiping out much of the human race. I refer of course to the so-called environmentalist movement.

All over Europe and the US, Marxists are joining the environmental movement. And no wonder: environmentalism is also a coercive utopianism — one as impossible to achieve as socialism, and just as destructive in the attempt.

A century ago, socialism had won. Marx might be dead, and Lenin still a frustrated scribbler, but their doctrine was victorious, for it controlled something more important than governments: it held the moral high ground.

Socialism was, they said, the brotherhood of man in economic form. Thus was the way smoothed to the gulag.

Today we face an ideology every bit as pitiless and messianic as Marxism. And like socialism a hundred years ago, it holds the moral high ground. Not as the brotherhood of man, since we live in post-Christian times, but as the brotherhood of bugs. Like socialism, environmentalism combines an atheistic religion with virulent statism. But it ups the ante. Marxism at least professed a concern with human beings; environmentalism harks back to a godless, manless, and mindless Garden of Eden.

If these people were merely wacky cultists, who bought acres of wilderness and lived on it as primitives, we would not be threatened. But they seek to use the state, and even a world state, to achieve their vision.

And like Marx and Lenin, they are heirs to Jean Jacques Rousseau. His paeans to statism, egalitarianism, and totalitarian democracy have shaped the Left for 200 years, and as a nature worshipper and exalter of the primitive, he was also the father of environmentalism.

During the Reign of Terror, Rousseauians constituted what Isabel Paterson called "humanitarians with the guillotine." We face something worse: plantitarians with the pistol.

Feminist-theologian Merlin Stone, author of *When God Was a Woman*, exults: "The Goddess is back!" The "voice of Gaia is heard once again" through a revived "faith in Nature."

Gaia was an earth goddess worshipped by the ancient Greeks, and James Lovelock, a British scientist, revived the name in the mid-1970s for "the earth as a living organism," an almost conscious self-regulating "biosphere."

There is no Bible or "set theology" for Gaia worship, says the Rev. Stone, when making a national tour of Unitarian churches. You can "know Her simply by taking a walk in the woods or wandering on the beach." All of Nature forms her scriptures.

"Industrial civilization is acne on the face of Gaia," says Stone, and it's time to get out the Stridex.

Ancient pagans saw gods in the wilderness, animals, and the state. Modern environmentalism shares that belief, and adds — courtesy of a New Age-Hindu-California influence — a hatred of man and the Western religious tradition that places him at the center of creation.

Environmentalism also has roots in deism — the practical atheism of the Enlightenment — which denied the Incarnation and made obeisance to nature.

Early environmentalist John Burroughs wrote: we use the word "Nature very much as our fathers used the word God." It is in Nature's lap that "the universe is held and nourished."

The natural order is superior to mankind, wrote ecologist John Muir more than a century ago, because Nature is "unfallen and undepraved" and man always and everywhere "a blighting touch." Therefore, said the human-hating Muir, alligators and other predators should be "blessed now and then with a mouthful of terror-stricken man by way of a dainty."

Christianity, adds ecologist Lynn White, Jr., "bears an immense burden of guilt" for violating nature. It brought evil into the world by giving birth to capitalism and the Industrial Revolution.

Since we must think of nature as God, says William McKibben, author of the best-selling *End of Nature*, every "man-made phenomenon" is evil. We must keep the earth as "Nature intended." To punish man's desecration, ecologist Edward Abbey urged anti-human terrorism in his influential novel, *The Monkey-Wrench Gang*. And the fastest-growing group in the Gaia liberation movement, EarthFirst!, uses a monkey wrench for its symbol.

Founded by David Foreman, former head lobbyist for the Wilderness Society, EarthFirst! engages in "ecodefense" and "ecotage," from spiking trees (which maims loggers) to vandalizing road-building machinery to wrecking rural airstrips. One of its goals is cutting the world's population by 90 percent, and it has even hailed AIDS as a help.

Foreman was convicted for conspiracy to blow up the pylons that carry high-power wires (using, I'm sure, environmentally safe explosives), but his example is powerful, even among the alleged non-radicals. One of the mainstream environmentalists, David Brower — former head of the Sierra Club and founder of Friends of the Earth — urged that land developers be shot with tranquilizer guns. He agrees with McKibben: human suffering is much less important than the "suffering of the planet."

We must be "humbler" toward nature and use technology like "bicycle-powered pumps," says McKibben — who lives on an expensive Adirondack farm. But he wants the rest of us "crammed into a few huge cities like so many ants" because it's best for the planet. We shouldn't even have children, for "independent, eternal, ever-sweet Nature" must be disturbed as little as possible.

McKibben does admit to one sin: he owns a 1981 Honda. But a man who lives a properly ascetic life is "Ponderosa Pine."

A life-long leftist, Pine — whose real name is Keith Lampe — was an apparatchik of the black-power Student Non-Violent Coordinating Committee (which didn't have many students or much non-violence) and a founder of the Yippie Party. He rioted at the 1968 Democratic Convention and has been arrested nine times for civil disobedience.

Converted by Allan Ginsberg to environmentalism, Pine split with his wife and twin sons. She had complained about his "Tibetan vocal energy science" — a continuous, hour-long, top-of-the-lungs shout each morning as an act of "communion with Mother Earth."

With his civil disobedience campaign against logging, and environmental news service, newspaper columns, and newsletter (he refers to paper, in other contexts, as "dead tree flesh"), Pine has been extremely influential, though there is some dissent about his demand that we go barefoot to be in "more intimate touch with the earth." David Brower goes further, denouncing the Pinian *nom de terre*; did he, Brower asks angrily, have "permission from the Ponderosa Pines to use their name"?

But even Brower agrees with the knotty Pine's crusade to collectivize the US, return us to a primitive standard of living, and use the Department of Defense to do it. "I want to change the military's whole focus to environmentalism," says Pine.

In the meantime, however, it is possible to do something good for the earth as your last act. A recent issue of *EarthFirst! Journal*, notes *Washington Times* columnist John Elvin, had some advice for the lifelorn. "Are you terminally ill with a wasting disease?" asks the *Journal*. "Don't go out with a whimper; go out with a bang! Undertake an eco-kamikaze mission."

> The possibilities for terminally ill warriors are limitless. Dams from the Columbia and the Colorado to the Connecticut are crying to be blown to smithereens, as are industrial polluters, the headquarters of oil-spilling corporations, fur warehouses, paper mills. ...

To those feeling suicidal, this may be the answer to your dreams. ... Don't jump off a bridge, blow up a bridge. Who says you can't take it with you?

Ron James, an English Green leader, says the proper level of economic development is that "between the fall of Rome and the rise of Charlemagne."

"The only way to live in harmony with Nature is by living at a subsistence level," as the animals do.

The normal attitude for most of human history was expressed by the Pilgrims, who feared a "hideous and desolate wilderness, full of wild beasts and wild men." Only a free society, which has tamed nature over many generations, enables us to have a different view.

"To us who live beneath a temperate sky and in the age of Henry Ford," wrote Aldous Huxley, "the worship of Nature comes almost naturally." But "an enemy with whom one is still at war, an unconquered, unconquerable, ceaselessly active enemy" — "one respects him, perhaps; one has a salutary fear of him; and one goes on fighting."

Added Albert Jay Nock, "I can see nature only as an enemy: a highly respected enemy, but an enemy."

Few of us could survive in the wilderness of, say, Yellowstone Park for any length of time (even though the environmentalists let it burn down because fire is natural). Nature is not friendly to man; it must be tempered.

Because they know that the vast majority of Americans would reject their real agenda, the environmentalists use lies, exaggerations, and pseudo-science to create public hysteria.

EXXON: The environmental movement cheered the criminal indictment of the Exxon Corporation for the Alaska oil spill, with the possibility of more than $700 million in fines. The one shortcoming, say the Sierra Club and the Natural Resources Defense Council, is that Exxon executives won't be sent to prison.

Exxon cannot be allowed to get away with an "environmental crime" which despoiled the "pristine wilderness of Alaska," says Attorney General Richard Thornburgh. But the legal doctrine underlying this indictment is inconsistent with a free society, notes Murray N. Rothbard.

Under feudalism, the master was held responsible for all acts of his servants, intended or not. During the Renaissance with growing capitalism and freedom, the doctrine changed so there was no "vicarious liability." Employers were correctly seen as legally responsible only for those actions they directed their employees to take, not when their employees disobeyed them. But today, we are back in feudal times, plus deeper-pocket jurisprudence, as employers are held responsible for all acts of their employees, even when the employees break company rules and disobey specific orders — by getting drunk on duty, for example. From all the hysteria, and the criminal indictment, one might think Exxon had deliberately spilled the oil, rather than being the victim of an accident that has already cost its stockholders $2 billion. Who is supposedly the casualty in the Justice Department's "criminal" act? Oiled sand?

In fact, Exxon is the biggest victim. Through employee negligence, the company has lost $5 million worth of oil, a supertanker, and compensation to fishermen, or the cost of the clean up. The total bill could be $3 billion.

Yet every night on television, we were treated to maudlin coverage of oily water and blackened seagulls, and denunciations of Exxon and oil production in "environmentally sensitive" Alaska. Though why it is more sensitive than, say, New Jersey, we are never told. In fact, environmentalists love Alaska because there are so few people there. It represents their ideal.

Despite all the hysteria, oil is — if I may use the environmentalists' own lingo — natural, organic, and biodegradable. As in previous oil spills, it all went away, and the birds, plants, and fish replenished themselves.

The Exxon oil spill was hardly the "equivalent of Hiroshima," as one crazed Alaska judge said. And who knows? Oil might be good for some wildlife. This year, the salmon catch is almost 50 percent bigger than any time in history.

WETLANDS: One of the great engineering achievements of the ancient world was draining the Pontine Marshes, which enabled the city of Rome to expand. But no such project could be undertaken today; that vast swamp would be protected as wetlands.

When John Pozsgai — an emigrant from communist Hungary — tried to improve some property he found this out. After buying a former junkyard and clearing away the thousands of tires that littered it, Pozsgai put clean topsoil on his lot in Morrisville, Pennsylvania. For this, the 57-year-old mechanic was sentenced to three years in prison and $200,000 in fines, because his property was classified as wetlands by the federal government.

After ordering a bureaucrat to "get the Hell off my property," Pozsgai was arrested, handcuffed, and jailed on $10,000 bail. Quickly tried and convicted, Pozsgai's brutal sentence will — said the prosecutor — "send a message to the private landowners, corporations, and developers of this country about President Bush's wetlands policy."

John Pozsgai has a different view: "I thought this was a free country," he told the *Washington Post*.

RUBBISH: In Palo Alto, California, citizens are ordered to separate their trash into seven neatly packaged piles: newspapers, tin cans (flattened with labels removed), aluminum cans (flattened), glass bottles (with labels removed), plastic soda pop bottles, lawn sweepings, and regular rubbish. And to pay high taxes to have it all taken away.

In Mountain Park, Georgia, a suburb of Atlanta, the government has just ordered the same recycling program, increased taxes 53 percent to pay for it, and enacted fines of up to $1,000, and jail terms of up to six months, for scofftrashes.

Because of my aversion to government orders, my distrust of government justifications, and my dislike of ecomania, I have always mixed all my trash together. If recycling made sense — economically and not as a sacrament of Gaia worship — we would be paid to do it.

For the same reason, I love to use plastic fast-food containers and non-returnable bottles. The whole recycling commotion, like the broader environmental movement, has always impressed me as malarkey. But I was glad to get some scientific support for my position.

Professor William L. Rathje, an urban archaeologist at the University of Arizona and head of its Garbage Project, has been studying rubbish for almost 20 years, and what he's discovered contradicts almost everything we're told.

When seen in perspective, our garbage problems are no worse than they have always been. The only difference is that today we have safe methods to deal with them, if the environmentalists will let us.

The environmentalists warn of a country covered by garbage because the average American generates 8 lbs. a day. In fact, we create less than 3 lbs. each, which is a good deal less than people in Mexico City today or American 100 years ago. Gone, for example, are the 1,200 lbs. of coal ash each American home used to generate, and our modern packaged foods mean less rubbish, not more.

But most landfills will be full in ten years or less, we're told, and that's true. But most landfills are designed to last ten years. The problem is not that they are filling up, but that we're not allowed to create new ones, thanks to the environmental movement. Texas, for example, handed out 250 landfill permits a year in the mid-1970s, but fewer than 50 in 1988.

The environmentalists claim that disposable diapers and fast-food containers are the worst problems. To me, this has always revealed the anti-family and pro-elite biases common to all left-wing movements. But the left, as usual, has the facts wrong as well.

In two years of digging in seven landfills all across America, in which they sorted and weighed every item in 16,000 lbs. of garbage, Rathje discovered that fast-food containers take up less than 1/10th of one percent of the space; less than 1 percent was disposable diapers. All plastics totalled less than 5 percent. The real culprit is paper — especially telephone books and newspapers. And there is little biodegradation. He found 1952 newspapers still fresh and readable.

Rather than biodegrade, most garbage mummifies. And this may be a blessing. If newspapers, for example, degraded rapidly, tons of ink would leach into the groundwater. And we should be glad that plastic doesn't biodegrade. Being inert, it doesn't introduce toxic chemicals into the environment.

We're told we have a moral obligation to recycle, and most of us say we do so, but empirical studies show it isn't so. In surveys, 78 percent of the respondents say they separate their garbage, but only 26 percent said they thought their neighbors separate theirs. To test that, for seven years the Garbage Project examined 9,000 loads of refuse in Tucson, Arizona, from a variety of neighborhoods. The results: most people do what they say their neighbors do — they don't separate. No matter how high or low the income, or how liberal the neighborhood, or how much the respondents said they cared about the environment, only 26 percent actually separated their trash. The only reliable predictor of when people separate and when they don't is exactly the one an economist would predict: the price paid for the trash. When the prices of old newspaper rose, people carefully separated their newspapers. When the price of newspapers fell, people threw them out with the other garbage.

We're all told to save our newspapers for recycling, and the idea seems to make sense. Old newspapers can be made into boxes, wallboard, and insulation, but the market is flooded with newsprint thanks to government programs. In New Jersey, for example, the price of used newspapers has plummeted from $40 a ton to minus $25 a ton. Trash entrepreneurs used to buy old newspaper. Now you have to pay someone to take it away.

If it is economically efficient to recycle — and we can't know that so long as government is involved — trash will have a market price. It is only through a free price system, as Ludwig von Mises demonstrated 70 years ago, that we can know the value of goods and services.

The cavemen had garbage problems, and so will our progeny, probably for as long as human civilization exists. But government is no answer. A socialized garbage system works no better than the Bulgarian economy. Only the free market will solve the garbage problem, and that means abolishing not only socialism, but the somewhat more efficient municipal fascist systems where one politically favored contractor gets the job.

The answer is to privatize and deregulate everything, from trash pickup to landfills. That way, everyone pays an appropriate part of the costs. Some types of trash would be taken away for a fee, others would be picked up free, and still others might command a price. Recycling would be based on economic calculation, not bureaucratic fiat.

The choice is always the same: put consumers in charge through private property and a free price system, or create a fiasco through government. Under the right kind of system, even I might start separating my trash.

McDONALDS: I've always admired McDonald's. It put restaurant dining within the reach of the average American, and made cross-country travel less of a culinary roulette. But these days, the gold on those arches is looking a little bit green.

For 15 years, McDonald's put its hamburgers in styrofoam boxes, and no wonder. The containers kept the food hot, clean, and dry, and the foam even absorbed grease.

Styrofoam was a wonderful invention, as anyone who's ever held a paper cup of hot coffee can testify. Light, strong, cheap, and insulating, styrofoam was a consumer godsend. So naturally, the environmentalists — whose declared enemy is the consumer society — despised it.

The Environmental Defense Fund persuaded McDonald's to ban styrofoam as "bad for the environment." By this, they do not mean the customers' environment, since paper leaves a hamburger cold and soggy much more quickly than styrofoam.

The environmentalists say that styrofoam doesn't biodegrade. But so what? Rocks don't biodegrade either. Why should we mind styrofoam buried under our feet as versus rocks? Because styrofoam is manmade, and therefore evil, whereas rocks are natural, and therefore good.

Non-ecological factors may be at work, however. Edward H. Rensi, president of McDonald's U.S.A., said the company can "switch to paper and save money." And if the customers don't like it? What are you, a spotted owl murderer?

But McDonald's may not be getting off so easily. The Audubon Society criticizes the deal, saying that "a lot more paper means a lot more pollution."

I guess the environmentalists won't be satisfied until McDonald's slaps the burger directly onto our outstretched hand. If it is a burger. An agreement with the animal rights movement may be next. Anyone for a McTofu?

Portland, Oregon — in a move that other cities are studying — has hired ex-New York bureaucrat Lee Barrett as a "styrofoam cop." Since January 1990, no restaurant or other retail food seller in Portland has been able to use products made of the wonderful insulating foam. It is Barrett's job to swoop down on businesses to make sure they are not styro-criminals. If they are, he can levy $250 fines for the dread offense — with $500 for hardened offenders.

ALAR: Just before the publication of a National Research Council study extolling fresh fruits and vegetables (why do government scientists get paid to repeat what our mothers told us?), and pooh-poohing the trivial pesticide residues on them, the environmentalists arranged an ambush.

A PR man for the Natural Resources Defense Council was featured on *60 Minutes*, points out syndicated columnist Warren Brookes, and Ed Bradley denounced Alar as the "most potent carcinogen in our food supply." This was disinformation.

Alar — used safely since 1963 — helps ripen apples, keeps them crisper, and retards spoilage. Using an EPA-mandated dosage 22,000 times the maximum intake of even an apple-crazy human, one rat out of the thousands tested developed a tumor. This was the extent of the "scientific proof" used not only to harm the manufacturer, Uniroyal, which had to pull Alar off the market, but the entire US apple industry.

A saner voice — Dr. Sanford Miller, dean of the medical school at the University of Texas at San Antonio — noted that "the risk of pesticide residues to consumers is effectively zero." But apple sales dropped, and apple growers lost more than $250 million, with many driven into bankruptcy.

Says Dr. Miller: 99.9 percent of the pesticide carcinogens now eaten by humans are natural. And as man-made pesticides and fungicides are banned, we are endangered. "Fungi produce the most potent carcinogens in nature."

RATS: The attack on Alar was based on rodent testing. And many other helpful products have been forced off the market, and companies and consumers harmed, through such panics. And now it turns out, as many of us have long thought, that such tests are defective.

Two recent articles in the journal *Science* — by Bruce Ames of the University of California, Berkeley, and Samuel Cohen of the University of Nebraska Medical College — have shown that it is the massive dose itself, no matter what the substance, that causes tumors.

The hyperdosages, explain these scientists, kill cells in the test animals, which their bodies then replace. The more this takes place over the animal's lifetime, the greater the chance of a cell mutation leading to cancer.

As with Alar, take thousands of rats and fill them full of a chemical for their whole lives, and it can be no surprise when one develops a tumor. This shows us that no one should try to live on Alar, but it tells us nothing about an infinitesimal residue, so small as to be barely measurable, of this helpful chemical.

GREENHOUSE: On the first Earth Day in 1970, environmentalists warned that we faced a new ice age unless the government took immediate and massive action. Today, using much of the same data, they claim we are endangered by global warming. These are the same climatologists who can't tell us whether it will rain next Friday, but who are certain the earth's temperature will be x degrees Celsius higher on a specific day in the future. Increased levels of carbon dioxide in the atmosphere will melt the polar ice caps and coastal areas will flood, we're told. As temperatures increase, Dallas will become a desert and Baked Alaska more than a dessert.

The proposed solution to this "Greenhouse Effect" is, surprise!, more government spending and control, and lower human standards of living. President Bush's budget has $375 million for greenhouse research.

Yet the "net rise in world surface temperature during the last century is about one degree Fahrenheit," nearly all of it before 1940, notes syndicated columnist Alton Chase. "And the northern oceans have actually been getting cooler. The much-vaunted 'global warming' figures are concocted by averaging equatorial warming with north temperate cooling."

A National Oceanographic and Atmospheric Administration study of ground temperature in the US from 1889 to 1989 found no warming. And a recently concluded ten-year satellite weather study by two NASA scientists at the Huntsville Space Center and the University of Alabama also found zero warming.

There is no evidence of global warming, but even if it were to take place, many scientists say the effect would be good: it would lengthen growing seasons, make the earth more liveable, and forestall any future ice age.

CLEAN AIR ACT: Bush's Clean Air Act, signed into law in October 1990, gives the EPA dictatorial power over every American business whose products might be harmful if burned. Since almost everything is toxic if burned, this is the establishment of Green central planning.

The bill also subsidizes ethanol, methanol, and compressed natural gas, and orders manufacturers to produce expensive cars that run on them.

Ethanol, a corn-based fuel beloved of Sen. Bob Dole (R-IRS) and his ethanol-producing mentor, Dwayne Andreas of Archer-Daniels-Midland, gives off other forms of pollution, and is much more expensive than gasoline. (Note: this provision, by artificially increasing this demand for corn, will also raise food prices by about $10 billion.)

Methanol is a highly corrosive fuel that destroys the normal automotive engine, requiring super-expensive alternatives. It costs more than gasoline, is only half as efficient, and is so toxic as to make gasoline seem almost benign in comparison.

Compressed natural gas requires massive steel tanks. A container holding the energy equivalent of a normal gasoline tank is much bigger and weighs 30 times as much, lowering mileage and wiping out most trunk space. And even a minimal number of refueling stations will cost $15 billion.

The Clean Air Act also has higher CAFE standards (fleet-wide economy regulations) that will have the effect of mandating lighter and therefore more dangerous automobiles.

The bill also places new and heavy regulations on hundreds of thousands of small businesses, in the OSHA tradition. OSHA is the quintessential Establishment regulatory agency, since the Exxons of the world can easily handle its depredations, while small businesses cannot. It has been a tremendous relative benefit to big business, and a barrier to entrepreneurs and small firms.

The new Clean Air Act replicates this, in spades. Any business using one of 200 common chemicals will have to undergo a lengthy and expensive licensing process. This includes your corner dry cleaner and print shop. And if the owner violates any regulations, knowingly or unknowingly, he will be subjected to heavy civil and even criminal penalties.

If a business gets new equipment, it will need a new permit — another bar to innovation for small companies. And if a factory changes its production method, it too will need a new permit. Again, this is no problem for Dow Chemical, only for Dow's would-be competitors.

As bad as all these provisions are, the most serious and expensive aspects of the Clean Air Act involve "acid rain" and the ozone layer.

ACID RAIN: Environmentalists are adept at PR, and the very name acid rain conjures up images of drops eating through your umbrella and dissolving your hair. In fact, it means only that litmus paper turns a different color.

The environmentalists tell us that America's streams, rivers, and lakes are becoming dangerously acidic, and that the villain is coal burning by utility companies. However, the government's own ten-year, $600 million National Acidic Precipitation Assessment Project — which the EPA has censored — found that acid rain is a non-problem.

Virtually all of the few acidic lakes have been that way since before the Industrial Revolution, thanks to water running through topsoil heavy with decaying vegetation. This is also why the naturalist Alexander von Humboldt found the giant Rio Negro river system in South America acidic and fishless 200 years ago.

Ironically, the fish in some Adirondack lakes — where there has been the most publicity — are affected by reforestation. Cutting down trees in the early part of the century led to less acidic soil, and a more neutral pH in the water, and artificially stocked fish thrived. Replanting over the last few decades has meant more acid.

OZONE: The other major focus of the Clean Air Act is the alleged deterioration of the ozone layer. We're told that we need a robust layer of ozone to prevent too much ultra-violet B radiation. But this is another non-problem. Since 1974, when we began measuring the UVB radiation level, it has declined 10 percent. Less is getting through, despite alleged anti-ozone chemicals.

Ozone is created by the action of sunshine on oxygen, so it should be no surprise that over the South Pole in the winter, when there is little sunshine, the ozone layer might thin, or even develop a temporary hole. This has happened, it is the only place it has happened, and it was first recorded in the mid-1950s, long before the alleged chemical villains were in significant use.

Ozone is harmed, we're told, by chlorofluorocarbons, the wonder chemicals used in air conditioners, refrigerators, and spray cans, and which are essential to the computer industry as well. Stable and non-toxic, CFCs cannot catch fire, and they are tremendously energy efficient. Yet the Clean Air Act will heavily tax, and eventually ban, all CFCs and related chemicals.

The planned substitutes are not only poisonous and energy inefficient, they can catch fire and even explode. The exploding refrigerator: it seems a perfect symbol of what the Clean Air Act, and the entire environmental movement, will inflict on us for the sake of the mythical Mother Nature.

But ozone is good, we're told, only in the upper atmosphere. To cut down on its incidence at street level in Los Angeles, the entire country will be fastened with additional anti-automotive and anti-industrial controls, with more bad economic effects.

A GREEN GNP?: The environmentalists feel they have a PR problem. Since their explicit agenda is to make us consume less, that is, to be poorer, they worry that this may not be popular. So they have a solution: the Green GNP.

GNP — gross national product — is already a deficient statistic. For example, as government spending grows, so does the GNP, even though government growth subtracts from real wealth. Nevertheless, as the statistical avatar of American business activity, the GNP has tremendous political significance.

To hide the fact that their legislation and regulation makes us poorer, the environmentalists want "environmental quality" incorporated into GNP. The Environmental Protection Agency and similar bureaucracies in Western Europe are funding research to make this possible.

The federal government already owns more than 40 percent of the United States. Say, under environmentalist pressure, another billion acres is taken out of production to save an endangered weed. Green accounting will claim that our environmental quality has been improved by x billion dollars, and add this to the GNP. Already, the GNP figures disguise how poor we're getting along, thanks to government intervention in the economy. A Green GNP will take us even further from reality.

SPOTTED OWLS: When I visited a logging area in far northern California, I found no environmentalists. As the Sierra Club's own studies demonstrate, environmentalists are upper-class types who live in places like Manhattan and Malibu, not in the woods. Those who do have no illusions about the Earth Goddess Gaia.

Loggers know that mankind's very existence depends on bending nature to our will, and that if we ever stop doing so, the jungle will reclaim our cities.

The livelihood of 30,000 working families in the Northwest will be destroyed by the Bush administration — approved anti-logging regulations on millions of acres, so 1,500 spotted owls can continue to live in the style to which they have become accustomed. If you think that wiping out 20 human families per owl seems excessive, it just shows how unenlightened you are.

(Note: if the spotted owl really is "endangered," and environmentalists want to save it, they should buy some land and set up an owl sanctuary. But using their own money somehow never occurs to them.)

The environmentalists privately admit, however, that the owl is not their major concern. It is outlawing all "old-growth" logging, a controversy which cuts to the heart of the environmentalist movement (unfortunately not with an ax).

Old-growth trees are precious because they were not planted by man, the Great Satan of the enviro-druidic religion. Pollution questions, although they make use of them, are irrelevant to these people. Old trees produce much less oxygen than new trees, so according to the "rainforest criterion," we should harvest all old trees and plant new ones. I don't notice any environmentalists recommending that, however. In fact, California had a Forests Forever ballot initiative defeated in November 1990, to ban all old-growth logging. These are the same people, remember, who wanted to let Yellowstone's trees burn down because the fire was started by natural lightning.

To drive through far northern California is to be reminded of the aptness of Ronald Reagan's "if you've seen one tree, you've seen them all" remark. The monotony is broken only by the occasional town, an oasis of civilization in a green desert. Yet the environmentalists would turn these into ghost cities. As one affluent environmentalist told me, "those people have no business living there." Now if I can only find an Audubon Society meeting so I can wear my new logger t-shirt: "I Love Spotted Owls. Fried."

OIL: With the US government prepared to go to war over oil, one would think that the environmental stranglehold on domestic energy production might be questioned. In fact, it has been made tighter, with millions more acres, offshore and within the US, forever barred — or so the environmentalists hope — from energy production for humans.

The Arctic National Wildlife Reserve is full of oil, perhaps eight to nine billion barrels worth — even more than Prudhoe Bay, points out columnist Stan Evans. So full of oil is this government wildlife reserve that oil seeps out of the ground and into the water, for some reason causing no media hysteria at the "desecration" involved. Yet this mammoth resource has been locked up by the feds through environmentalist pressure.

Production off the California, North and South Carolina, and Florida coasts is also banned, although there is probably 30 billion barrels there.

Through a coalition of rich people in places like Santa Barbara who don't want their free views disturbed by a distant drilling platform, and environmentalists who feel drilling contaminates Mother Earth, and might injure a seagull, the American people have been made poorer.

All federal lands should be privatized, but so long as they are government owned, they should at least be opened to productive human use, including oil production, coal and other forms of mining, and tree harvesting.

SMOKING: In 1604, James I of England ordered his subjects to stop using tobacco, "the horrible Stydgian smoke of the pit that is bottomless." Other anti-smoking politicians have tried whippings in Russia, nose-slittings in India, and beheadings in Turkey. One anti-smoking sultan roamed the streets of Istanbul in disguise and beheaded any tobacco seller he found. Even our present-day fanatics wouldn't go that far. I don't think.

Massachusetts outlawed the sale of tobacco in the 1630s, and in the 1640s, Connecticut banned public smoking and ordered private smokers to get a license.

These measures failed, just as Turkish capital punishment had. It was more than 150 years, points out our Gordon Dillow, before the anti-smoking movement revived.

All during the nineteenth century, what were called anti-smoking "agitations" increased. Eugenicist Orson Fowler even condemned it as an aphrodisiac, and warned that those who "would be pure in your love-instinct" should "cast this sensualizing fire from you."

In 1984, the *New York Times* said that "the decadence of Spain began when the Spaniards adopted cigarettes." With Americans using them, "the ruin of the Republic is close at hand."

Tobacco was accused of causing color blindness, weak eyesight, baldness, stunted growth, insanity, sterility, drunkenness, impotence, sexual promiscuity, mustaches on women, and constipation.

In 1893, New York Schools Commissioner Charles Hubbell said that:

> many and many a bright lad has had his will power weakened, his moral principle sapped, his nervous system wrecked, and his whole life spoiled before he is seventeen years old by the detestable cigarette. The "cigarette fiend" in time becomes a liar and a thief. He will commit petty thefts to get money to feed his insatiable appetite for nicotine. He lies to his parents, his teachers, and his best friends. He neglects his studies and, narcotized by nicotine, sits at his desk half stupefied, his desire for work, his ambition, dulled if not dead.

By 1909, with the help of the Woman's Christian Temperance Union, the National Anti-Cigarette League succeeded in outlawing smoking in North Dakota, Iowa, Tennessee, Wisconsin, Nebraska, Arkansas, Illinois, Kansas, Washington, South Dakota, and Minnesota. New York City outlawed smoking by women, and 29-year-old Katie Mulcahey was jailed for lighting up in front of a policeman and telling him: "No man shall dictate to me."

When drinking was outlawed, evangelist Billy Sunday said: "Prohibition is won; now for tobacco." The Presbyterian, Northern Baptist, and Methodist churches called for tobacco prohibition, but amidst growing public dismay about the effects of alcohol prohibition, they failed to win many more converts.

A popular song seemed to sum it all up:

Tobacco is a dirty weed. I like it.
It satisfies no normal need. I like it.
It makes you thin, it makes you lean, It takes the hair
    right off your bean.
It's the worst darn stuff I've ever seen.
I like it.

Gradually the states repealed their anti-tobacco laws. Kansas's was the last to go in 1927.

But tobacco prohibition fever is upon us once again. California always seems to lead the way in these matters, and today, not only do they have hectoring state anti-drinking signs in their restaurants, they are subjected to an expensive and intrusive state advertising campaign against smoking.

The anti-smoketeers were bolstered in the last decade by the Ruritanian admiral with the 1,000-mile stare, Dr. C. Everett Koop. As surgeon general, he preached about the dangers of "second-hand" smoke. But where was the evidence?

An American Cancer Society study of 180,000 American women has not detected any increased risk to non-smoking wives of heavy smokers. And a Yale Medical School study showed that tobacco smoke in the air very slightly improved the breathing ability of asthmatics!

But none of this matters. Our health Nazis are obsessed by the idea that someone, somewhere, might be enjoying a smoke or a drink. Therefore their $28.6 million government ad campaign.

I find the notion of state behavioral advertising chilling. (Although I wouldn't mind trying anti-bribe ads in the legislature.)

No one was supposed to be persuaded by the slogans that used to festoon Moscow: "Glory to the Communist Party," "Toil for the

Motherland," etc. They were there to demoralize the opposition. So it is in California.

With newspaper, TV, and radio ads, the state department of health services says it will "change the image" of smoking from "sexy, glamorous, youthful" to "dumb, dirty, dangerous." While I don't know anyone who thinks smoking is the former, the latter sounds like a great description of the California government.

The tobacco industry works through persuasion. The State of California (not to speak of the US government) gets its money, and its way, at the point of a gun. Give me Virginia Slims over the tax man any day.

SIEG HEALTH: We've always known the Nazis were economic left-wingers (Nazi standing for National Socialist German Workers Party), but now — thanks to Robert N. Proctor's *Racial Hygiene: Medicine Under the Nazis* (Harvard University Press, 1988) — we know they were health nuts, exercise freaks, ecologists, organic food zealots, animal righters, and alcohol and tobacco haters.

Like today's environmentalists, who place every bug and weed above humans, the Nazis were ardent conservationists. They passed a host of laws to protect "nature and nature's animals," especially "endangered" plants and animals.

The Nazis outlawed medical research on animals, with Hermann Göring threatening anyone who broke the law with being "deported to a concentration camp." He jailed a fisherman for six months because he cut off a bait frog's head while it was still alive, and the German humor magazine *Simplicissimus* ran a cartoon with a platoon of frogs giving Göring the Nazi salute.

As believers in "organic medicine," the Nazis urged the German people to eat raw fruits and vegetables, since the preservation, sterilization, and pasteurization of food meant "alienation from nature."

They even hated Wonder Bread. "In 1935, Reich's Health Führer Gerhard Wagner launched an attack on the recent shift from natural whole-grain bread to highly refined white bread," says Proctor. Denouncing white bread as a "chemical product," Wagner linked the "bread question" to a "broader need to return to a diet of less meat and fats, more fruits and vegetables, and more whole-grain bread."

In 1935, Wagner formed the Reich Whole-Grain Bread Committee to pressure bakers not to produce white bread, and Goebbels produced a propaganda poster tying Aryanism to whole-grain bread. In 1935, only 1 percent of German bakeries were health-food stores. By 1943, 23 percent were.

The Nazis were also anti-pesticide, with Hitler's personal physician, Theodore Morell, declaring the DDT especially was "both useless and dangerous." He prevented its distribution.

The Nazis funded massive research into the environmental dangers of background radiation, lead, asbestos, and mercury. They campaigned against artificial colorings and preservatives, and demanded more use of organic "pharmaceuticals, cosmetics, fertilizers, and foods." Government medical journals blamed cancer on red meat and chemical preservatives.

Drinking was actively discouraged, and there were stiff penalties for anyone caught driving drunk, with the police — for the first time — empowered to give mandatory blood alcohol tests.

Hitler, a vegetarian and health-food enthusiast, was also a teetotaler. Himmler shared Hitler's hatred for alcohol, and had his SS promote the production of fruit juices and mineral water as substitutes.

Hitler especially hated smoking, however, and he would allow no one to smoke in his presence. When the state of Saxony established the Institute for the Struggle Against Tobacco at the University of Jena in 1942, he donated 100,000 RM of his own money to it. He also banned smoking on city trains and buses.

The Nazis believed in natural childbirth, mid-wifery, and breastfeeding, and women who breastfed their children instead of using "artificial formula" received a subsidy from the state. By the middle 1930s, the Nazis had outlawed physician-assisted births in favor of midwives.

The Nazis also promoted herbal medicine, and the S.S. farms at Dachau were billed as the "largest research institute for natural herbs and medicines in Europe."

No wonder our eco-leftists have that glint in their eye. From now on, I'm going to check if they are wearing armbands.

One of the fastest growing and most radical parts of the environmental movement is the animal rightists. They too worship nature, but make a cult out of animals whom they equate with human beings, and in fact place above us.

BABY SEALS: About ten years ago, we were subjected to a barrage of photos and news stories about big-eyed seal pups hunted for their fur. Greenpeace stirred a worldwide propaganda campaign, and the European Community and others banned the import of the pelts.

This not only wiped out the livelihood of the natives who hunted the seals, but it harmed the fishing industry. With no hunting to keep the seal population under control, the animals are devouring increasingly scarce fish and damaging nets.

Some bureaucrats are proposing a government seal hunt (no private hunters, of course), but the environmentalists have prevented it. Meanwhile, stocks of cod and other fish continue to drop. Do the environmentalists care? We "shouldn't eat anything with a face," one told me.

FLIPPED OUT: One environmentalists' Victim of the Month was the dolphin. Some of the animals were caught inadvertently by tuna fishermen, but *Flipper* reruns on TV must have convinced millions of Americans that dolphins are intelligent, so the environmentalists were able to persuade them to spear the tuna industry.

Santa Barbara, California, has now declared a Dolphin Awareness Day; school children all across America engaged in letter-writing campaigns (those who still could, despite the government schools); and San Francisco kids were denounced if they brought tuna sandwiches to school.

The Audubon Society, the Humane Society, the Society for the Prevention of Cruelty to Animals, Greenpeace, People for the Ethical Treatment of Animals (PETA), and a host of similar organizations wanted an end, in effect, to the organized American tuna industry, and they may get it.

The Marine Mammal Protection Act, passed by Congress and signed by President Reagan in 1981, imposed convoluted regulations on the industry in the name of saving dolphins. But that's not good enough, said then-Congresswoman Barbara Boxer (D-CA): dolphins "have creative centers larger than humans." Or at least larger than members of Congress. So new federal restrictions are needed.

Even before the politicians could act, however, Greenpeace and other environmental groups pressured the four major tuna companies to stop using fish caught by nets because an occasional dolphin might be caught. The livelihood of American tuna fishermen, with the life savings of whole families invested in expensive boats and equipment, was, of course, irrelevant. The companies will now only buy tuna from the western Pacific, where there are no dolphins, and no American fishermen.

The environmentalists admit, be it noted, that they also cherish the life of the tuna, and want it also protected from fishermen, but they will have to wait. Charlie hasn't had his own TV show yet.

EXTINCTION: From the snail darter to the furbish lousewort, every existing animal and plant species must be kept in existence by the government — claim the environmentalists — even if human rights are violated. But why?

Most of the species that have existed since the "creation," from trilobites to dinosaurs, are now extinct through normal processes. Why not allow this to continue?

If, for scientific or entertainment purposes, some people want to preserve this species or that on their own land and at their own expense, great. Zoos and universities do this already. But the rest of us should not be taxed and regulated, and have our property rights wiped out, to save every weed and bug. The only environmental impact that counts is that on humans.

FUR: In Aspen, Colorado, voters defeated a proposed ban on fur sales, but in most places it is the furaphobes who make themselves felt, especially since they are willing to use almost any tactic.

They spray-paint women in fur coats, slash coats with razors and burn down fur stores. Last year, they put incendiary bombs in the fur-selling areas of department stores all over the San Francisco Bay area. Police suspect the Animal Liberation Front (ALF), which has been charged with using identical devices elsewhere. But such is the environmentalist influence in the media that there was little publicity.

ALF, which the California attorney general calls a terrorist organization, says it seeks "to inflict economic damage on animal torturers," from fur sellers to medical researchers.

MEDICAL RESEARCH: A physician researching Sudden Infant Death Syndrome, Dr. John Orem, "conducted ground breaking — and painless — research on cats," notes Katie McCabe in the *Washingtonian*, "until his lab was trashed by the Animal Liberation Front." Children may die as a result, but ALF says: so what? Anything is justified to stop the use of animals.

Congress listens respectfully to animal-rights lobbyists, and has passed legislation making medical research more expensive. One amendment from then-Sen. John Melcher (D-MT) requires researchers to protect the "psychological well-being" of monkeys (whom Congressmen must feel close to) at an estimated cost of $1 billion.

This plays, however, directly into the hands of people-killers. Who knows how many cures will go undiscovered because of these restrictions? Thousands of babies have been saved because we know about the Rh factor, which was discovered through the use of rhesus monkeys. But animal rights advocates say it is better that babies die than that monkeys be used to save them.

Even former Rep. Bob Dornan (R-CA) pushed animal-rights legislation that would add billions to medical research costs. Not that he goes all the way with these people. Although named "Legislator of the Year" by the radical PETA, Dornan still "wears leather shoes." Until PETA outlaws them, that is, for the animal rightists see cow leather as no different than human skin.

Fred Barnes reported in the *New Republic* — itself pro-animal rights — that the Bush administration buckled under animal rights pressure (Barbara is rumored to be a supporter) and "strongly opposed" legislation empowering the FBI to investigate terrorist attacks on medical research facilities.

In a cover story on the subject, *New Republic* senior editor Robert Wright says he was converted by the "stubborn logic" of the animal-rights movement, although he — like Dornan — doesn't go all the way. He still believes in "the use of primates in AIDS research."

ANTS AND SWANS: The animal rights lobby wants them to outlaw any use of animals in medical research, food, or clothing. There is "no rational basis for saying that a human being has special rights," says Ingrid Newkirk, director of PETA. "The smallest form of life, even an ant or a clam, is equal to a human being."

The "murder of animals," says Alex Pacheco, chairman of PETA, is equivalent to the "murder of men." Eating oysters on the halfshell makes you Charles Manson.

Recently there was an uproar in southern Connecticut. The state's wildlife division had proposed, in the face of an out-of-control swan population, to "shake eggs." The swans — large, heavy, aggressive birds with no natural predators in the area — were attacking children. The swans couldn't, of course, be hunted, so rangers were deputized to rattle fertilized eggs to prevent hatching.

Thousands of residents protested this violation of the swans' rights, many proponents of human abortion among them. If children were injured by the swans, so be it. (Note: This is in the Green tradition. Rousseau abandoned his five children as "an inconvenience" and animal-rights activists are typically pro-abortion.)

Let's get serious, says a PETA spokeswoman: "Six million Jews died in concentration camps, but six billion broiler chickens will die this year in slaughter houses."

From FDR to the present, the Democrats have been bad on environmentalism. It played an important part in the New Deal and the Great Society (Lyndon Johnson called himself "the Conservation President"), and any day I expect to see the Democrats designate trees as what Joe Sobran calls an Officially Accredited Minority, with a certain number of seats (plastic, of course) in their national convention.

But environmentalism got its political start under the original liberal Republican: Teddy Roosevelt. As no one who knows Washington will be surprised to learn, there were special interests at work.

When the federal government established the national parks system, and locked up millions of acres, it made other land — held especially by the timber and railroad interests associated with J.P. Morgan, Roosevelt's mentor — much more valuable. Some of these interests were the funders of the original conservation lobbying organization.

Richard Nixon continued this tradition when he established — by executive order — the Environmental Protection Agency. Not surprisingly, the EPA's budget has been dominated by sewage-treatment and other construction contracts for well-connected big businessmen. But small and medium businesses, and the American consumer, have suffered from its endless regulations.

And the head of the EPA was to be elevated by President Bush — the "Environment President" — to sit with the cabinet. President Bush also proposed a New Deal-style $2 billion program to plant a billion saplings, none of them members of Congress.

Are we short of trees? No, but the president is "genuinely fond of trees," says a White House aide. And although no one thinks it will "cure the Greenhouse effect," it's "symbolic of his commitment to the environment." American foresters, farmers, landowners, and homeowners don't know the proper number of trees, but Washington, DC, does.

Some problems, like alleged global warming, are so enormous, say the environmentalists, that only world government can solve them. And the one-world-types who infest the national Democrats and the resurgent Rockefeller wing of the Republican Party were glad to comply.

The State Department and the EPA negotiated a plan, based on the new Clean Air Act, to issue pollution permits worldwide. Third World countries would get "excess" permits, which they could then sell to Western companies, bringing about another transfer of wealth from the West to the Third World, which will undoubtedly be used to pay back the big bank loans of Third World governments.

Establishmentarian Elliot L. Richardson, writing in the *New York Times*, said that "nothing will be done" environmentally "without an institutional mechanism to develop, institute, and enforce regulations across national boundaries."

To build "a global Environmental Protection Agency," perhaps run like "the United Nations General Assembly," that could levy taxes and impose controls to make sure there is "equitable burden sharing," the US government must lead the way in the "interest of the entire world community."

Ever since Woodrow Wilson, liberals have been infected with the idea of world government. With the melding of the European Community and the coming establishment of its tax authority and central bank, the Trilateralist ideal has come closer.

Patriotic Americans must reject this globaloney, and not only on grounds of national sovereignty. We know how difficult it is to deal with city hall, let alone the state or federal government. A world bureaucracy would be a taxing, meddling nightmare. Well-connected international lawyers like Elliot Richardson would do well, but the average American would get it in the neck.

Once we reject utopianism, and realize that — for example — eight million people can't live in Los Angeles and have air like rural Colorado's — we can set about solving real environmental problems through the only possible mechanism: private property and the price system.

When the price system functions freely, it brings supply and demand into rough equality, ensuring that resources are put to their most-valued uses. To the extent that government meddles with prices, it ensures waste, hampers entrepreneurship, and makes people poorer.

If coffee — for whatever reason — becomes scarcer, its price goes up, which tells consumers to drink less. If more coffee comes on the market, its price goes down, telling consumers they can drink more. Prices thus constitute a system of resource conservation.

But environmentalists pretend — like Soviet central planners — to know economic values without prices. They claim we are "running out" of everything, and thus we need government controls on consumption. But if we really were running out of, say, oil, its price would skyrocket, telling consumers to use less and entrepreneurs to seek substitutes. And when the oil supply was threatened by the Iraqi War, that's exactly what happened.

Neither do the voluntary eco-restrictions work as intended. The environmentalists are forever telling us to be poorer and use less water, less gasoline, less toilet paper, etc. But if they reduce their consumption, it lowers the price for the rest of us, and we can use more. (P.S.: Don't pass this on to the environmentalists; it's the one favor they do the rest of us.)

When anything is commonly owned — like air and water — we see all the bad effects of socialism. People abuse the resource because they do not have to bear the price.

To solve this problem, anyone who is personally harmed, or his business damaged, by air pollution ought to be able to sue to stop it, and receive damages. But the federal government intervened in this common-law process in the nineteenth century to favor special interests, making it impossible, to take a real example, for a farmer to sue a railroad whose spark emissions burned down his orchard.

The federal government also nationalized the coasts and waterways specifically to smooth the way for industrial special interests.

If, as is the case with many waterways in England and other countries, people had property rights in the streams and rivers running through their land, they could prevent pollution just as they prevent trash-dumping in their front yard. And if fishermen and homeowners held property rights in the coasts and adjacent waters, they could prevent pollution and properly allocate fishing rights.

The recent hysteria over African elephant tusks was another problem of property rights. If people were allowed to raise elephants and sell their tusks — as even the Zimbabwean government pointed out — there would be no more and no fewer elephant tusks than there should be. The same principle applies to all other resources. If left in common ownership, there will be misuse. If put in private hands, we will have the right amount: supply will meet demand.

An example of market conservation was the Cayman Turtle Farm in the British West Indies. The green sea turtle was considered endangered, thanks to over-harvesting due to common ownership. The Farm was able to hatch eggs and bring the hatchlings to maturity at a far higher rate than in nature. Its stock grew to 80,000 green turtles.

But the environmentalists hated the Cayman Turtle Farm, since in their view it is morally wrong to profit from wildlife. The Farm was driven out of business and the green turtle is again on the endangered species list.

Greens — like all liberals — justify government intervention because of what economists call "public goods" and "externalities."

A "public good" is supposed to be something we all want, but can't get, unless government provides it. Environmentalists claim everyone wants national parks, but the market won't provide them, so the government must. But how can we know, independent of the market, that everyone does want these expensive parks? Or how many parks of what sort?

We could take a survey, but that doesn't tell us the intensity of economic demand. More important, it is not enough to know that people want, for example, diamonds. That means something economically only if they are willing to give up other things to obtain them.

Amazingly, liberal economists have never developed a way to identify these so-called public goods, so-objective scientists that they are-they use intuition. Paul Samuelson's favorite example was the lighthouse, until Ronald Coase demonstrated that private entrepreneurs had provided lighthouses for centuries.

If we realize that only the market can give us economic information, the alleged problem of public goods disappears. Absent government prohibitions and subsidies, or competition from "free" parks, the market will ensure that we have exactly the number and type of parks that the American people want, and are willing to pay for. Moreover, if we sell all the national parks, we can pay off the federal debt.

An "externality" is a side-effect. Your neighbors' attractive new landscaping is a positive externality; their barking dog is a negative one. One is a blessing, the other an irritant, but you voluntarily purchase neither.

Environmentalists say, for example, that trash is a negative externality of consumerism. So they advocate more regulation and bureaucracy to solve it. Yet the free market solves this much more justly and efficiently through property rights. Privatize everything and the externalities are "internalized," that is, those who ought to bear the costs do. But to environmentalists, human prosperity is itself a negative externality.

Chicken or chicory, elephant or endive, the natural order is valuable only in so far as it serves human needs and purposes. Our very existence is based on our dominion over nature; it was created for that end, and it is to that end that it must be used — through a private-property, free-market order.

The environmental movement is openly anti-human and virulently statist. Is it any coincidence that the Nazis exalted animals, nature, and vegetarianism above humans, civilization, and civilized eating, or that our environmentalists have an air of green goose step about them?

The environmentalists must be opposed — if they will excuse the expression — root and branch. But it will not be easy.

Unfortunately, the environmentalists have company in assaulting our freedom. Under the guise of protecting freedom, the State has tried to seize control of our children and to destroy family authority.

Christopher Ratte, professor in the department of classics at the University of Michigan, was recently turned into a jailbird and had his son taken away from him, all in the name of protecting the child from the father. He had taken his seven-year-old son to a baseball game in Detroit and ordered him lemonade. What was served up was a "Mike's Hard Lemonade," which his son prepared to drink. Suddenly security arrived.

"You know this is an alcoholic beverage?" the security guard asked.

"You have got to be kidding," responded the professor. And before the professor could examine the bottle, the guard snatched it away, and the boy was taken to the hospital where no traces of alcohol were found in him. The boy was then promptly put in foster care. It was two days before the mother, a professor of architecture, was allowed to take him home, and a full week before the father was allowed to come back into the home again.

The case provides a remarkable look at the workings of bureaucracy. The *Detroit Free Press* interviewed all the people involved. It turns out that no one was happy about what happened, but the gears of the bureaucracy ground away, ruining peoples' lives for no good reason.

The cop on duty thought it was a mistake, but his supervisor was insisting that he act. When Child Protective Services came to take the child away into their cruel foster care, the police objected. But CPS was just doing its duty. It had no choice but to take the child since the police had requested a court order — also triggered by events — to remove the child. Observers who know the system say that the only surprising aspect to this case is that child was returned so quickly. Had the couple been poor, uneducated, and unconnected, the case might still be tied up in the courts.

The lesson many people draw from this is that social workers are being given too much authority, that governments need to be reformed so that they do not take extreme measures too hastily, that cops need to use good sense before busting up families, etc. The problem is that all of these reforms ultimately depend on the state to use its discretionary power judiciously.

The real issue concerns the locus of control. Does it belong to the family or the state? When there is a dispute, to whom does the presumption of innocence belong? It is not enough to say: here is a bad family environment, so of course the state should control the outcome. When it comes to the power of the state over the family, there is no such thing as a judicious use. The state has every reason to invent reasons to destroy families — and all other independent centers of authority — and the families themselves have no choice but to crawl and beg.

State campaigns for the welfare of children have always been a major justification for the expansion of leviathan. This is the primary basis for the war on drugs, which has robbed us of so many civil liberties. It is the basis for the nationalization of education that is taking place, administration by administration, in the name of preventing any child from being left behind. If the Interent is ever regulated in the US the way it is in China and parts of Europe, it will be in the name of protecting the children. Indeed, it is possible to erect a totalitarian state in the name of helping the children.

So it was in Texas, when the state swept in to remove 437 children from their mothers. The police were responding to a call claiming abuse, but there was no other basis for this incredible action than the desire to crush a religion completely. The state decided the dissident church shouldn't exist, and so it claimed all power in the interest of the children. The state could count on sympathy from mainstream American culture, which rightly disapproves of polygamy and underage marriages. And that is precisely why the group separated themselves completely from the rest of the culture.

Should people be free to set up cults, to live undisturbed to practice their religion, to deviate from mainstream ethical codes? Certainly if we believe in freedom, people should be able to do this. In fact, the group was already under a great deal of pressure to reform from the outside and inside, with former members of the group reporting despotic control by the leader and many men who had been excommunicated putting pressure on those inside to leave. We don't know whether the entire matter — if indeed abuse was taking place — might have been handled in this way, because the state intervened to impose the cruelest possible solution: namely, taking children from their mothers' arms and putting them in the hands of government social workers.

In the name of protecting children, the state already runs a huge program with government officials posing as teenagers seeking sex and arresting those who fall for the scam. By itself, this is very strange, with government becoming a source for the very problem that government is trying to correct. Meanwhile, a February–March 2008 report from the *American Psychologist* reports that the fears about Interent predation are wildly exaggerated and do not reflect the facts. This is hardly a surprise, since the state has incentive to exaggerate the pathologies of society as a means of getting a clawhold over every independent sector.

The goal of the state is to find some practice that is universally reviled and pose as the one and only way of expunging it from society. The best example today is child pornography, a grim and ghastly industry that every decent person would like to see eradicated from the earth. But in the name of doing so, the state invades everyone's privacy, controls speech, interferes with families, and otherwise uses the issue as a wedge to undermine every freedom.

Thus do we see what is wrong with statements such as the following:

> We have an obligation to protect children from sexual exploitation and abuse, and we can do this by increasing communication between state and federal agencies to help combat this repulsive industry. While privacy rights should always be respected in the pursuit of child pornographers, more needs to be done to track down and prosecute the twisted individuals who exploit innocent children.

Do we really want to unleash the state to solve this problem? Not if we understand the dynamics of statism. The power will not be used to solve the problem, but rather to intimidate the population in ways to which people will find it difficult to object. The trouble is that the above words were not written by the typically naïve do-gooder, social worker, or Justice Department bureaucrat. They were penned by spokesmen for the Libertarian Party.

Thus can we see the power of propaganda, and its uses. Not even self-identified libertarians can see that state authority over the family is a basis for the loss of liberty in our time, and that the state always poses the greater threat to society than whatever problem it purports to solve. There is a further problem: a concession that the state can indeed solve social problems that cannot be corrected without the state, is to give up the entire argument over the future of liberty itself.

The environmentalist movement portrays humanity as the enemy of the earth and sides against humanity; and its influence of the State, as we've seen, is vast. There's another important area in which the State makes war on large sections of humanity. The State bears primary responsibility for racism.

What is racism and how can we tell if it exists? I'm not talking about someone who dislikes African-Americans or whites or Latinos. We might call that racism on the level of individual ethics, but there are no inevitable and widespread social consequences of a bad attitude. Defining racism, a notion highly charged with political implications, also raises the specter of the Thought Police: did you or did you not think politically incorrect thoughts?

Let's deepen and broaden the discussion in light of what Ludwig von Mises says about racism in contrast to the liberal view of the social order. In *Omnipotent Government*, he shows that the modern doctrine of racism originated with the Frenchman Joseph Arthur Comte de Gobineau as a way to justify aristocratic privilege. In the hands of the Nazis, the doctrine was extended to the alleged superiority of Aryans over everyone else. They claimed that the races were inherently incompatible, and advocated state policies to bring about their desired outcome.

Mises first regards racism as a particular species of a general social theory that posits the existence of intractable conflicts in society, and that therefore it is impossible for society to work properly absent some fundamental structural change brought about by the state. In the old Marxist variety, this conflict was between capital and labor. That view doesn't have many adherents anymore since real-world events have disproved the Marxian vision for more than a century. The poor didn't get poorer under capitalism; they became richer than ever before in human history.

In a similar way, the racialists must also confront the reality of the market economy. As Mises said, in a market economy, there is no legal discrimination against anyone. Freedom prevails, and "whoever dislikes the Jews may in such a world avoid patronizing Jewish shopkeepers, doctors, and lawyers." The problem is that this does not produce the results racists want. Indeed, the market always tends to bring people together in peace, neither compelling nor forbidding exchanges.

"Many decades of intensive anti-Semitic propaganda did not succeed in preventing German 'Aryans' from buying in shops owned by Jews, from consulting Jewish doctors and lawyers, and from reading books by Jewish authors." What the racists wanted required more. "Whoever wanted to get rid of his Jewish competitors could not rely on an alleged hatred of Jews; he was under the necessity of asking for legal discrimination against them."

The end result, then, is a policy of interventionism. This interventionism is required if a racist result is to be brought about, and the allegedly intractable conflict finally resolved. If this logic is carried to its end point, the result is mass suffering and death. The Jews were the problem in Germany, so they had to be eradicated. The Kulaks in Russia similarly had to be destroyed. Same with anyone with Western or bourgeois attachments in Mao's China or Pol Pot's Cambodia. The Hegelian synthesis in each of these cases is achieved through mass slaughter. The supposedly persistent conflict between groups is washed away in rivers of blood.

Even as Marxists abandoned their old view of capital-labor relations, they promoted the conflict view of society — one entirely at odds with the old liberal idea — in other forms. This is because the Marxian view itself has deeper roots in Hegel's view that history must tend toward a synthesis of two opposing forces, culminating in some transforming moment. Socialism is one way to render the Hegelian view in material terms. But there are other ways. So long as you have the perception of a war-to-the-knife conflict, history cries out for a resolution.

Thus does the Marxian view easily mutate to take on a different cast depending on the political moment. The sexist view of the world, for example, holds that men and women have opposing interests, and that a gain by one sex always comes at the expense of the other. A forced rearrangement of social institutions, they believed, was required to fix the problem.

Now, keep in mind that this view of society is not necessarily held by one group or another. We think of anti-male women's activists who believe that women can only advance through political action, but the view can also be held by men. The misogynist male might also believe that women are the key problem with the world, and so social structures need to be forcibly rearranged to favor men.

The conflict view is a part of the environmentalist agenda too. The notion that humans cannot advance without killing nature is widely held today. People look at China's advancing economy and their first thought is not human flourishing, but environmental catastrophe. Think too of those who accept as an article of faith that changes in weather patterns are due to us humans living it up too much.

We see this further today in the area of religion. Some people are dead set on the idea that a free society is incompatible with a multiplicity of religious faiths. This view is particularly popular among Christian fundamentalists, who claim that Islam will never be satisfied until it wipes out Christianity, and that every new mosque is a mortal threat to Christendom. They can't imagine that people can co-exist in peace, tolerance, and trade, leaving religion to personal conscience.

So too with race. Decades after Gobineau, in the 1930s, it became the intellectual fashion to believe that state eugenics was necessary to cull the population of its inferior elements, so that the superior elements could thrive. Behind this was an elaborate argument about human evolution and the need for planned reproduction. This view was widely held on the left and the right, in highbrow and lowbrow circles. Why was state planning necessary? Because, it was believed, there was a genetic competition that pitted all racial groups against all, and only one group could win.

Thus did the racialist view resemble Marxism, changing the posited conflict from capital and labor to the races. What the racialists failed to understand, or understood but hated, was the capacity for voluntary institutions to harmonize racial interests. The United States showed this to be true. After the ghastly civil war came the blessed abolition of slavery, and then the end of laws requiring racial segregation. We saw how the free market can bring about cooperative trading relationships among all people. (Of course, the laws hindering freedom of association and contract in the name of anti-racism retarded social cooperation.)

What freedom has illustrated is that differences among people do not need to lead to intractable conflicts. More and more social cooperation is possible and fruitful, to the extent that people are granted the freedom to associate, trade, make contracts, and work together toward their mutual advantage.

Sadly, however, among many people in this country, there is still the impression that state-mandated institutional change, even revolution, is required to end intractable conflicts. They believe that the very essence of the social structure captures this racial conflict. Some blacks hold this view, some whites hold this view, some Latinos hold this view — the ideology of racism does not elude any group.

It should be no surprise, then, that Mises's ideas have drawn fire from white racialists who insist that by talking about markets and freedom, we are evading the real issue, which is who will dominate. And there is the view that prosperity is not really about the question of freedom, but about the purity of the genetic stocks. Such views are not limited to whites; black activists too speak as if the only issue that really matters is gaining legal preferences for their group. In either case, the agenda is all about who has power over whom, rather than ending the ability of any group to have power over any other group.

The state is not a neutral observer. It will pass environmental legislation. It will regulate relations between races and sexes. It will put down this religion in order to raise that one up. In each case, the intervention only exacerbates conflicts, which in turn creates the impression that there really is an intractable conflict at work. For example, if the state taxes one group to give to another group, it fuels conflict and gives the impression that legislation is the route to liberation.

But who is the real winner in this game? The state and the state alone. By purporting to be the great social referee, it accumulates more power unto itself and leaves everyone else with less freedom to work out their own problems. And here is the real problem with racism or any -ism that fails to understand the capacity of the free society to work out its own problems through exchange and mutual benefit.

Thus can we see that racism is not a unique problem in society but part of a larger misconception about the basis of social cooperation.

Do you ever travel by air? Then of course you have met the TSA. If you have boarded an airplane recently, you know something about how the state lives in a strange, alternative universe in which good sense, normal courtesies, and sound judgment play no role. No aspect of life is perfect, but the sectors the state manages are wacky and topsy-turvy.

Thus we are expected to believe that every living person who boards an airplane is a potential terrorist, and every person is just as much a risk as every other person. We are expected to believe that because the state forces us to carry deodorant in a little baggy, that we are safer from hijackings than we would otherwise be. We are supposed to gain comfort when we see a TSA employee testing a tube of toothpaste to make sure that it won't explode on board.

It is all so ridiculous, and oddly alarming. If there is one thing we can know for sure, it is that a regular terrorist is not going to subject himself to these petty investigations. The source of trouble will be completely unexpected. The bureaucrats only do what they are told to do, and those making the rules have no financial incentive to decouple authentic from bogus threats.

As Judge Napolitano has noted, the TSA's measures are stupid and do not succeed in keeping us safe. "But how does confiscating water bottles, snow globes, and 'toy transformer robots' while waving deadly weapons and diseases through the gates, protect our security?"

Intrusive searches are by no means confined to airplane passengers, Napolitano points out. The New York Police Department, along with many other police departments across the country, now conducts random bag searches in the subway, without suspicion or warrant, in order to prevent terrorist attacks. These random searches clearly violate the Fourth Amendment, which is meant to protect all persons from warrantless searches and seizures. If you are unlucky enough to be selected "randomly," the officers will stop you as you hurry to catch your morning train. As the doors slide closed on the platform below and your train departs, you stand helplessly as the bored cops search your bag.

A federal appeals judge ruled that these searches were constitutional.

In August 2006, Judge Chester Straub of the United States Court of Appeals for the Second Circuit ruled that the NYPD acted within the law because the subway bag searches fell within the "special needs exception" to the Fourth Amendment due to imminent terrorist threats.

Napolitano mordantly comments, "There is no 'special needs' exception in the Fourth Amendment. The court simply made it up."

These searches are of course only a small part of the so-called "War on Terror." The Patriot Act and other laws and Executive Orders allow the government to pry into the correspondence, telephone calls, and financial records anyone it chooses to classify as a possible sympathizer with terrorism. You might think that this applies to only a few extremists and has nothing to do with ordinary Americans. If you think this, you are in for a surprise.

If you're a member of an activist organization or have ever blogged about how betrayed you feel by your government, or how you really wish they would end this futile war and bring your kid home from Iraq, your name might be on the terrorist watch list along with thousands of other innocent people. Your phone might be tapped, your computer might be monitored, and thousands of surveillance cameras may be focused on you as you trip over that crack in the sidewalk. Today more than ever, Big Brother may be watching.

If he is watching, then, Napolitano reminds us, the Patriot Act allows him to enlist involuntarily the services of members of the public to assist in spying. Further, a citizen thus drafted into service is forbidden, under criminal penalties, to disclose that he has received a National Security Letter.

The Patriot Act places a gag order on any person served with:

> a self-written search warrant ... for information, barring them from disclosing that the FBI has either sought or obtained information from them. If a town librarian tells a neighbor ... that the government has taken her Internet browsing records, the innocent librarian can end up in a federal prison for five years because of her truthful speech.

Isn't this an outrageous interference with our right of free speech?

Assaults on liberty, today as in the past, are supported on the grounds that security must be protected. But the defenders of these measures fail to show that they in any way do improve our security. In what way, e.g., did the internment of Japanese Americans during World War II aid the American war effort? Napolitano remarks that it took more than 30 years for the American government to apologize for this outrageous policy. One wonders whether in years to come the government will issue a new apology for the many acts of tyranny of the Bush administration.

Robert Higgs remarks about the Patriot Act,

> Our rulers declare that by nothing more substantial than the emperor's say-so, any person may be arrested and held incommunicado, without trial, and then punished, even put to death. Say good-bye to the writ of *habeas corpus*, the very bedrock of limited government. ... Do I [Higgs] fear that the USA PATRIOT Act will be abused? No. I know that it has been already and will continue to be as its elastic language allows unscrupulous prosecutors to scratch a variety of itches unrelated to terrorism.

The extent to which the War on Terror violates our freedom is truly frightening. Bush claimed to be completely above the law and to have the power to imprison or kill anyone he wished, including American citizens, with no legal safeguards whatever.

That outstanding civil libertarian attorney Glenn Greenwald has characterized the situation we face in this way:

> [P]rior to the December 2005 disclosure that President Bush had violated the law, no one ever suggested that the FISA [Foreign Intelligence Surveillance Act] framework impeded necessary eavesdropping. If anything, the FISA court had long been criticized ... for being too permissive, for allowing the government whatever eavesdropping powers it requested. Indeed, its reputation for granting every eavesdropping request made by the government is so widespread that it has long been ridiculed as the "Rubber Stamp Court." ... The FISA court approved every single request [out of 13,102 submitted between 1978 and 2001] and only modified the requested warrant on a grand total of two occasions.

Why then did the Administration bypass the court? Greenwald responds:

As Congress devised the law, the FISA court plays two critical, independent functions — not just warrant approval but also, more critically, judicial oversight. FISA's truly meaningful check on abuse in the eavesdropping process is that the president is prevented from engaging in improper eavesdropping because he knows that every instance of eavesdropping he orders will be known to a federal judge — a high level judicial officer who is not subject to the president's authority ... it is precisely that safeguard which President Bush simply abolished by fiat. In effect, President Bush changed the law all by himself, replacing the federal judges with his own employees at the NSA [National Security Agency] and abolishing the approval and warrant process entirely.

Bush ignored the court, in sum, because he thinks that he possesses plenary powers in all matters that concern security. But how can he think this? Doesn't the Constitution grant the president only strictly limited powers? No one can reasonably question this; but, as Greenwald notes, some legal theorists have done just that. Notoriously, John Yoo, a Berkeley law professor who served as deputy assistant attorney general, wrote an extraordinary memorandum on September 25, 2001:

Yoo contended that the president's powers were not confined only to battlefields or wars; he emphatically argued that the president has the power to make any decisions with regard to all matters relating to defense and that neither the Congress, nor the courts, nor any long-standing laws can restrict or limit those decisions in any way.

As Greenwald makes clear, Bush has applied his claim to be above the law far beyond the issue of wiretaps. Bush has acted on the belief that he may seize anyone, even an American citizen living within the United States, and hold him as he deems fit in a military prison, there to be subject to harsh treatment that really amounts to torture. Yaser Hamdi, an American citizen, was seized by the American Army in Afghanistan in 2001.

In secret, President Bush signed a decree accusing Hamdi of being an "enemy combatant" and ordered his administration to keep Hamdi in a military prison. Hamdi was not charged with any crime and was not allowed access to a lawyer. He was simply locked away and allowed no contact with anyone, and the administration asserted the right to detain Hamdi under these circumstances *indefinitely*.

When the Supreme Court rejected the administration's claim, Hamdi was deported to Saudi Arabia.

Even worse, José Padilla, also an American citizen, was arrested on American soil and cast into a military prison.

On June 9, 2002, President Bush signed yet another secret order, this one decreeing Padilla to be an enemy combatant, and as a result, he was transferred to a military prison in South Carolina and subjected to the same "black hole" treatment that Hamdi received — placed in solitary confinement, not formally charged with any crime, denied access to a lawyer.

Once more, the administration claimed that it was free to do anything it wanted to an American citizen in the name of defense. When it appeared that the Supreme Court was about to rule on the constitutionality of this claim to dictatorial power, the administration transferred Padilla to the civilian authorities; he was then tried in court and convicted. The treatment he received in military prison had meanwhile made him mentally ill.

Even if Congress passes a law that forbids the use of torture, Yoo and his associates contend that the president is not bound by its terms: once more, he possesses plenary powers in matters of defense. The president has brazenly issued "signing statements" when he approves new legislation that declare that he will interpret laws in accord with his own dictatorial conception of his powers, i.e., he will disregard the law when it suits him.

As Ron Paul noted in a speech to Congress on November 29, 2001:

> The target of our [congressional] efforts has sadly been the liberties all Americans enjoy. With all the new powers we have given the administration, none has truly improved the chances of catching the terrorists who were responsible for the 9/11 attacks. All Americans will soon feel the consequences of this new legislation. ... Laws recently passed by Congress apply to all Americans, not just terrorists.

I'm sorry to say that the situation is even worse. President Obama claims the authority to kill American citizens without trial, if he deems them sufficiently dangerous, and he has done just that. Anwar-al-Awlaki, an American-born Muslim cleric, was killed in a drone attack. As William Norman Grigg explains,

The links connecting Anwar al-Awlaki to anti-American terrorism were entirely suppositious, forged through unsubstantiated official assertion. He was, at most, a clerical propagandist who never exercised command authority. For that matter, no evidence has been presented that he ever had an operational role in a military force of any kind.

Awlaki — an American-born cleric who was once courted by the Pentagon — was accused of expressing support for armed attacks against US military personnel and government interests. It is not terrorism to employ lethal violence against an invading and occupying army, nor is it a crime to express support for armed self-defense — including armed interposition against the aggressive designs of the U.S. government.

The administration asserted — without providing evidence — that Awlaki had an "operational" role in planning terrrorist attacks against U.S. citizens. If evidence supporting that charge existed, the administration had the unconditional constitutional duty to indict Awlaki and put him on trial.

The vertically integrated murder apparatus that killed Awlaki and fellow U.S. citizen Samir Khan is entirely autonomous — and increasingly automated. Awlaki was added to a "kill list" and his execution "sanctioned" by a secret legal memorandum, on the basis of things he had said in public. Within a few years, the machinery of mass murder will be refined to the point where people — including U.S. citizens — may find themselves targeted for execution on the basis of behavior "patterns" that suggest unexpressed but impermissible thoughts.

Ron Paul reacted with appropriate indignation: "That's not a good way to deal with our problems," he said of the drone strike in Yemen that killed Awlaki.

"He was born here," said Paul. "He is an American citizen. He was never tried or charged with any crime. Nobody knows if he killed anyone."

And Paul said the precedent of striking against Americans, even those suspected of being terrorist masterminds, is not a good one.

"If the American people accept this blindly and casually — have a precedent of an American president assassinating people who he thinks are bad. I think that's sad," he said.

The government, beyond a doubt, is engaged in war against American citizens. Once more, we shouldn't think that the government's assault affect only a few outliers. Government efforts to watch everybody aren't confined to measures ostensibly directed at terror suspects. Judge Napolitano calls attention to another intrusion — cameras installed to catch speeders. Relying on these cameras denies due process to the accused:

> The tickets are practically indisputable, since the images of the vehicle are not close enough to capture the driver of the vehicle. If the license plate recorded is registered to you, you're guilty. Period. These cameras are so profitable that in Britain they are referred to as "yellow vultures" and are the most lucrative cameras in the country.

Napolitano notes that using these cameras increases accidents, since drivers speed up at intersections in an effort to avoid detection; nevertheless, the cameras are increasingly part of the local scene in various sections of America.

The aim of the government seems to be to subject everybody to total surveillance. If what you do is always under the eye of a government agent, then the government is in position at once to stifle any resistance to its plans for us. The government's aim here was prefigured by the Panopticon project of the British utilitarian Jeremy Bentham. Murray Rothbard describes Bentham's plan in this way:

> In visiting his brother Samuel in Russia, in the 1780s, Bentham found that his brother had designed such a panopticon, as a workshop, and Bentham immediately got the idea of the Panopticon as the ideal physical site for a prison, a school, a factory — indeed, for all of social life. "Panopticon," in Greek, means "all-seeing," and the name was highly suitable for the object in view. Another Benthamite synonym for the panopticon was "the Inspection House." The idea was to maximize the supervision of prisoners/school children/paupers/employees by the all-seeing inspector, who would be seated at a tower in the centre of a circular spider-web able to spy on all the cells in the periphery. By mirrors and other devices, each of the spied-upon could never know where the inspector was looking at any given time. Thus the panopticon would accomplish the goal of a 100 per cent inspected and supervised society without the means; since everyone could be under inspection at any time without knowing it.

Bentham's apologists have reduced his scheme to merely one of prison "reform," but Bentham tried to make it clear that all social institutions were to be encompassed by the panopticon; that it was to serve as a model for "houses of industry, workhouses, poorhouses, manufactories, mad-houses, lazarettos, hospitals, and schools." An atheist hardly given to scriptural citation, Bentham nevertheless waxed rhapsodic about the social ideal of the panopticon, quoting from the Psalms: "Thou art about my path, and about my bed; and spiest out all my ways ..."

Bentham's goal was to approach, or simulate, the "ideal perfection" of complete and continuous inspection of everyone. Because of the inspector's "invisible eye," each inmate would conceive himself in a state of total and continuing inspection, thus achieving the "apparent omnipresence of the inspector."

Of course, Bentham didn't originate the idea of the government keeping tabs on its citizens. That idea has a long historical precedent. Since the Middle Ages, the State has used the census as an instrument of control.

"There went out a decree from Caesar Augustus," says St. Luke on why Mary and Joseph found themselves in Bethlehem, "that all the world should be taxed." Joseph had to go to his own city because the tyrannical Roman government was conducting a census. But the information may have been used for more than just taxation. The Roman government's local ruler later decided he wanted to find the Christ child and kill Him.

Did the government make use of census data to find out where the members of the House of David were? We can't know for sure, although a later Roman despot did. But we can know that Joseph made a huge error in obeying the census takers in the first place. They were up to no good. In fact, another group of religious Jews in Judea decided that they would not comply with the Roman government's demand to count and tax them. The group was known as the "Zealots" (yes, that's where the word came from). They saw complying with the census as equivalent to submitting to slavery. Many ended up paying for their principled stand with their lives.

And yet, their resistance arguably made would-be tyrants more cautious. For ten centuries after Constantine, when feudal Europe was broken up into thousands of tiny principalities and jurisdictions, no central government was in a position to collect data on its citizens. This is one of the many great merits of radically decentralized political systems: There is no central power that controls the population through data gathering and population enumeration.

The only exception in Europe in those years was William the Conqueror who, after 1066, attempted to establish in England a centralized and authoritarian society on the Roman model. That meant, in the first instance, a census. The census was compiled in *The Domesday Book*, Domesday meaning the day of reckoning or last judgment, so named by an Anglo-Saxon monk because it represented the end of the world for English freedom.

A predecessor to today's tax rolls, it functioned as a hit list for the conquering state to divide property up as it wished. "There was no single hide nor yard of land," read a contemporary account, "nor indeed one ax nor one cow nor one pig was there left out, and not put down on the record." Eventually the attempt to keep track of the population for purposes of taxes led to the Magna Carta, the foundational statement of limits on the state's power.

The Domesday Book established the precedent for many other attempts at compiling information. But according to Martin Van Creveld (author of *The Rise and Decline of the State*, 1999), the information-gathering techniques of these times were so primitive, and the governments so decentralized, that the data were largely useless. On the Continent, for example, no government was in the position of demanding a comprehensive census. That began to change in the sixteenth century, when the nation-state began to gain a foothold against the countervailing power of the church, free cities, and local lords. In France, the first modern philosopher of the state, Jean Bodin, urged that a census be taken to better control the people.

Also in France, writes Voltaire, Louis XIV tried but failed to develop a comprehensive accounting of "the number of inhabitants in each district — nobles, citizens, farm workers, artisans and workmen — together with livestock of all kinds, land of various degrees of fertility, the whole of the regular and secular clergy, their revenues, those of the towns and those of the communities." It turned out that this was just a utopian fantasy. Even if the Sun King could have devised the form, it would have been impossible to force people to surrender all that information.

The first censuses of the eighteenth century were taken in Iceland and Sweden using depopulation as an excuse. But America after the revolution of 1776 faced no such problem, and the generation that complained of British tax agents knew better than to invest government with the power to collect information on citizens. In the Articles of Confederation, drafted in the days of full revolutionary liberty, each state had one vote, no matter how many representatives it sent to Congress. There was no demand for a census because the central government, such as it was, had no power to do much at all.

It was with the US Constitution in 1787 that the real troubles began. The document permitted more powers to the federal government than any free person should tolerate (as Patrick Henry argued), and the inclusion of a census was evidence of the problem. The framers added the demand for a census in the interests of fully representing the people in the legislature, they said. They would have two legislative houses, one representing the states and the other the people in the states. For the latter, they would need a head count. Hence, the government would count heads every ten years.

Why else was a head count needed? Article I, Section 2, included an ominous mention of taxes, recalling not only Caesar Augustus but the whole tyrannical history of using the census to control people:

> Representatives and direct Taxes shall be apportioned among the several States which may be included within this Union, according to their respective Numbers, which shall be determined by adding to the whole Number of free Persons, including those bound to Service for a Term of Years, and excluding Indians not taxed, three-fifths of all other Persons. The actual Enumeration shall be made within three Years after the first Meeting of the Congress of the United States, and within every subsequent Term of ten Years, in such Manner as they shall by Law direct.

The 1790 census seemed innocent enough, but by 1810, matters already were out of control: For the first time, the government started demanding information on occupations. Fortunately for the American people, the records were burned by the British in 1813, leaving hardly a trace for the state to use to expand its power. And yet, the state would not be held back, and the census became ever more intrusive.

The lesson of the history of the US census is this: Any power ceded to a government will be abused, given time. Today, the long-form of the census asks for details of your life that you would never tell a neighbor or a private business. A total of 52 questions, some outrageously intrusive, appear on it.

Every census is worse than the last. The 1990 census asked for the year of your birth, but the 2000 census wants to know the day and the month, not to mention the race and relation of every person in the house, along with the number of toilets and much more. And what is this information used for? Mostly for social and economic central planning — an activity the government shouldn't be engaged in at all.

This isn't a biased rendering of the objectives of the census. The Census Bureau itself says, "Information collected in Census 2000 will provide local area data needed for communities to receive federal program funds and for private sector and community planning." You only have to ask yourself what any eighteenth- or nineteenth-century liberal would have thought of the idea of "private-sector" and community planning undertaken by the central state.

Indeed, very few Americans trust their government enough to allow it to engage in planning. Consider the incompetent Census Bureau itself. The letters it sent out in advance of the forms put an extra digit in front of the addresses, as the head of the bureau admitted in a Feb. 26 press release, while trying to blame it on someone else. And these are the people we are supposed to trust to gather information on us to plan our lives? No thanks.

The letter from the government says, "Census counts are used to distribute government funds to communities and states for highways, schools, health facilities and many other programs you and your neighbors need." In short, the purpose is no different from that of William the Conqueror's: to redistribute property and exercise power. Clearly, we've come a long way from the head-counting function of the census. Moreover, there are quite a few of us out here who don't believe that we "need" these programs.

What's worse, the point of the original census was not to apportion a fixed number of House members among the states. It was rationally to expand the number of people serving in the House as the population grew. But after the Civil War, the number of House members stopped growing, so there's not much point to the census at all now — or at least no purpose consistent with liberty.

Moreover, if a head count were all that was needed, the job could be done by using data from private companies or the US Postal Service. But the census wants more than that. Why? Forget all the official rationales. The real reason the government wants the information is to control the population. The promises that the data won't be used at your expense is worth the same as all government promises: zippo.

What is a freeman supposed to do when he receives the form in the mail? First, remember that information is the foundational infrastructure of the would-be total state. Without it, the state is at a loss. And then consider whether the costs associated with noncompliance are outweighed by the subjective benefit one receives from joining with all free people in resisting the government's data-collection efforts. Finally, consider the limited purposes for which the Framers sought to use the census, and ask yourself whether the central government of today really can be trusted with knowing what is better kept to yourself.

For many years, voluntary compliance has been falling. In anticipation of this problem, the Census Bureau has been relying on wholly owned sectors of society to propagandize for its campaign. The *Sesame Street* character named Count von Count is touring public schools to tell the kids to tell their parents to fill out the census, even as more than one million census kits have been sent to public schools around the country. Think of it as the state using children to manipulate their parents into becoming volunteers in the civic-planning project.

It is a bullish sign for liberty that the government only achieved 65 percent mail-in compliance in 1990. And given the decline in respect for government that characterizes the Clinton era, you can bet it will be even lower today. If you do choose to fill out the census, some commentators have recommended you adhere strictly to the Constitution and admit only how many people live in your household. That such a tactic is considered subversive indicates just how far we've come from eighteenth-century standards of intrusion.

In 1941, Gustav Richter, an aide to Adolf Eichmann, was sent to Romania to gather information about the Jewish population in a census, with the ultimate goal of plotting a mass deportation to the Belzec concentration camp. But Romania cut off all political relations with the Nazis and, as a result, the Jewish population was spared the fate of Jews in Poland and Austria. Just as the Zealots of the first century knew, when a government seeks information on people, it is up to no good.

When the government keeps tabs on us, it of course does so not just to amass information. Those of us who defy its wishes are in grave danger of imprisonment. Americans, perhaps like all people, have a remarkable capacity for tuning out unpleasantries that do not directly affect them. I'm thinking here of wars on foreign lands, but also the astonishing fact that the United States has become the world's most jail-loving country, with well over 1 in 100 adults living as slaves in a prison. Building and managing prisons, and locking people up, have become major facets of government power in our time, and it is long past time for those who love liberty to start to care.

Before we get to the reasons why, look at the facts as reported by the *New York Times*. The US leads the world in prisoner production. There are 2.3 million people behind bars. China, with four times as many people, has 1.6 million in prison. In terms of population, the US has 751 people in prison for every 100,000, while the closest competitor in this regard is Russia with 627. I'm struck by this figure: 531 in Cuba. The median global rate is 125.

What's amazing is that most of this imprisoning trend is recent, dating really from the 1980s, and most of the change is due to drug laws. From 1925 to 1975, the rate of imprisonment was stable at 110, lower than the international average, which is what you might expect in a country that purports to value freedom. But then it suddenly shot up in the 1980s. There were 30,000 people in jail for drugs in 1980, while today there are half a million.

Other factors include the criminalization of nearly everything these days, even passing bad checks or the pettiest of thefts. And judges are under all sorts of minimum sentencing requirements. Now, before we move to causes and answers, please consider what jail means. The people inside are slaves of the state. They are captured and held and regarded by their captors as nothing other than biological beings that take up space. The delivery of all services to them is contingent on the whims of their masters, who have no stake in the outcome at all.

Now, you might say that this is necessary for some people, but be aware that it is the ultimate assault on human dignity. They are "paying the price" for their actions, but no one is in a position to benefit from the price paid. They aren't working off debts or compensating victims or struggling to overcome anything. They are just "doing time," costing taxpayers almost $25,000 a year per person. That's all these people are to society: a cost, and they are treated as such.

And the communities in which they exist in these prisons consist of other un-valued people, and they become socialized into this mentality that is utterly contrary to every notion of civilization. Then there are the relentless threat and reality of violence, the unspeakable noise, the pervasiveness of every moral perversity. In short, prisons are Hell. It can be no wonder that they rehabilitate no one. As George Bernard Shaw said, "imprisonment is as irrevocable as death."

What's more, everything we know about government applies to this ultimate government program. It is expensive (states alone spend $44 billion on prisons every year), inefficient, brutal, and irrational. The modern prison system is also a relatively new phenomenon in history, one that is used to enforce political priorities (the drug war) rather than punish real crimes. It is also manipulated by political passions rather than a genuine concern for justice. The results of the drug war are not to reduce consumption but rather the opposite. Illegal drugs are now a $100 billion dollar industry in the US, while the drug war itself costs taxpayers $19 billion, even as the costs of running the justice system are skyrocketing (up 418 percent percent in 25 years).

People say that crime is down, so this must be working. Well, that depends on what you mean by crime. Drug use and distribution are associated with violence solely because they are illegal. They are crimes because the state says they are crimes, but they do not fit within the usual definition we find in the history of political philosophy, which centers on the violation of person or property. What's more, the "crime" of drug use and distribution hasn't really been kept down; it has only gone further underground. It's a major irony and commentary on the workability of prisons that drug markets are very active there.

Now to causes. Some social scientists give the predictable explanation that all this is due to the lack of a "social safety net" in the US. In the first place, the US has had such a net for a hundred years, and yet these people seem not to have noticed, even though no such net is big enough for some people. Moreover, it is more likely the very presence of such a net — which creates a moral hazard so that people do not learn to be responsible for their own well-being — that contributes to criminal behavior (all else being equal).

There are those on all sides who attribute the increase to racial factors, given that the imprisoned population is disproportionately black and Hispanic, and noting the disparity in crime rates in such places as Minnesota with low levels of minority populations. But this factor too could be illusory, especially as regards drug use, since it is far more likely that a state system will catch and punish people with less influence and social standing than those whom the state regards as significant.

A more telling point comes to us from political analysts, who observe the politicization of judicial appointments in the United States. Judges run on their "tough on crime" records, or are appointed for them, and so have every incentive to lock people up more than justice truly demands.

One factor that hasn't been mentioned so far in the discussion is the lobbying power of the prison industry itself. The old rule is that if you subsidize something, you get more of it. And so it is with prisons and the prison-industrial complex. I've yet to find any viable figures on how large this industry is, but consider that it includes construction firms, managers of private prisons, wardens, food service providers, counselors, security services, and a hundred other kinds of companies to build and manage these miniature societies. What kind of political influence do they have? Speculation here, but it must be substantial.

As for public concern, remember that every law on the books, every regulation, every line in the government codebook, is ultimately enforced by prison. The jail cell is the symbol and ultimate end of statism itself. It would be nice if we thought of the interests of the prisoners in society and those that will become so. But even if you are not likely to be among them, consider the loss of privacy, the loss of liberty, the loss of independence, the loss of all that used to be considered truly American, in the course of the building of prison nation.

But won't crime go up if we abandon our prison system? Let Robert Ingersoll answer:

The world has been filled with prisons and dungeons, with chains and whips, with crosses and gibbets, with thumb-screws and racks, with hangmen and headsmen — and yet these frightful means and instrumentalities and crimes have accomplished little for the preservation of property or life. It is safe to say that governments have committed far more crimes than they have prevented. As long as society bows and cringes before the great thieves, there will be little ones enough to fill the jails.

Even if you manage to avoid being sent to jail, you are likely to at some time or other encounter the police. If so, you have a good chance of encountering violence and total disregard for your rights. As Gary Chartier notes, military veterans, trained in violence in Iraq and elsewhere, often find jobs in domestic police forces. Their training all-too-often makes them treat Americans as enemy combatants. "Military organizations and high-pressure combat-linked environments can encourage the dehumanization of perceived enemies. And people can bring their histories with them into civilian life."

Of course, if people have guns and other weapons, the power of the government over them is not complete. The conclusion is obvious: the government must take away our guns. So far, it has been unable to do so, but Obama's cynical manipulation of the Sandy Hook shootings makes his intentions obvious.

Joyce Lee Malcolm's outstanding book *Guns and Violence: The English Experience* shows us what the gun controllers have in mind, through a detailed account of what they have done in Britain. By studying the British experience with gun control, we can see what is in store for us.

Her detailed study of British legislation on the topic shows the real aim of the disarmers. They wish to abolish the right to armed self-defense entirely. The point is not only to block armed resistance to the state, as I had previously thought; in addition, everyone is to be made totally dependent on the state for protection.

Some of Malcolm's examples are shocking. In England:

[m]erely threatening to defend oneself can also prove illegal, as an elderly lady discovered. She succeeded in frightening off a gang of thugs by firing a blank from a toy gun, only to be arrested for the crime of putting someone in fear with an imitation firearm.

Not even if one's life is in danger can one legally use a weapon. In another case, two men assaulted Eric Butler in a subway, smashing his head and choking him. "In desperation he unsheathed a sword blade in his walking stick and slashed at one of them. ... The assailants were charged with unlawful wounding but Butler was also tried, and convicted of carrying an offensive weapon."

You can imagine the legal position if someone goes so far as to use a real gun to defend himself. As British law now stands, you cannot even use a gun in your own home to defend yourself against burglars. In a 1999 incident, Tony Martin surprised a professional burglar and his accomplice while they robbed his home. He fired, killing one of them.

Did the government commend Martin for his bravery in confronting the burglars? Quite the contrary, they tried and convicted him for murder. "Thus an English farmer, living alone, has been sentenced to life in prison for killing one professional burglar and ten years for wounding another when the two broke into his home at night." Fortunately, our story has a "happy" ending: the court of appeals reduced his sentence to five years, on grounds of "diminished capacity."

Supporters of gun control, I suspect, will not be moved by these cases. "However unfair it seems to punish someone for defending himself," they will claim, "we have no choice. We must reduce violence in society. The state cannot protect everyone, and curtailment of the right to self-defense will cause innocent people to suffer." But so what? Doesn't a slogan from a once prominent regime tells us that the common good goes before individual good? If we insist on the outdated ideas of personal rights and responsibilities, we will end up as a Wild West society like the United States, where guns are plentiful and violent crime flourishes. The "horror stories" just recounted took place in England, where as everyone knows, the curbs on private ownership of weapons have caused violent crime to occur far less often than in America. Down with the right to self-defense!"

Malcolm's outstanding book thoroughly demolishes the case for gun control just sketched. She proceeds by a learned study of violent crime in England, from the Middle Ages to the present. In her survey, a constant theme emerges. As guns became more prevalent, violent crime decreased. This trend culminated in the nineteenth century, when death by murder was rare but guns were widespread. The seizure of guns during the twentieth century has been accompanied by a marked increase in violent crime. At present some types of violent crime are more common in England than in America. As usual, the statists have their facts exactly backward.

Often people think of English medieval life as relatively calm and peaceful, but in Malcolm's view this is a myth. "Medieval England was boisterous and violent, more so than court records reveal. ... This high rate of homicide and violent crime existed when few firearms were in circulation."

Malcolm's interest in the Middle Ages is not confined to her primary theme of the relation between guns and violence. She introduces another theme that will concern her throughout the book: the status of the right to self-defense. During this period, custom and law established the right of individuals to resist violence directed against them. In some instances, a person who killed his assailant stood immune from criminal penalty. I will mention just a few highlights from Malcolm's detailed narrative. The Tudor and Stuart periods, "this era in which firearms first came into common use in everyday life as well as for the citizen militia ... in which the Englishman's right to have 'arms for his defence' was proclaimed, also witnessed a sharp decline in violent homicide."

Developments in the eighteenth century should by now come as no surprise. "[A]t the very time that the individual right to be armed was becoming well established and guns were replacing earlier weapons, the homicide rate continued its precipitous decline."

Readers will not earn a reward for correctly guessing Malcolm's conclusions about the nineteenth century. Once again, the number of guns increased while violent crime declined. "The nineteenth century ended with firearms plentifully available while rates of armed crime had been declining and were to reach a record low."

So far, we have a vast example of an inductive argument. Increases in the prevalence of guns have always accompanied decreases in violent crime. Does this not strongly suggest that guns in private hands deter crime? The twentieth century, especially its latter half, gives us a chance to test our induction, since ownership of guns during that period came under strict control.

And of course violent crime did increase.

> Scholars of criminology have traced a long decline in interpersonal violence since the late Middle Ages until an abrupt and puzzling reversal occurred in the middle of the twentieth century ... a statistical comparison of crime in England and Wales with crime in America, based on 1995 figures, discovered that for three categories of violent crimes — assaults, burglary, and robbery — the English are now at far greater risk than Americans.

The gun controllers of course will counter what we have said by repeating over and over, "guns are dangerous." Rothbard shows what's wrong with their claim:

> It should be clear that no physical object is *in itself* aggressive; *any* object, whether it be a gun, a knife, or a stick, can be used for aggression, for defense, or for numerous other purposes unconnected with crime. It makes no more sense to outlaw or restrict the purchase and ownership of guns than it does to outlaw the possession of knives, clubs, hatpins, or stones. And how are all of these objects to be outlawed, and if outlawed, how is the prohibition to be enforced? Instead of pursuing innocent people carrying or possessing various objects, then, the law should be concerned with combatting and apprehending real criminals.

4

THE BANKERS' WAR ON AMERICA: THE FED

DECEMBER 23, 2013 MARKED 100 years since Congress authorized the creation of the Federal Reserve System. Throughout that century the Fed has enjoyed broad bipartisan support. That's another way of saying the Fed never appeared on the political radar until Ron Paul broke the rules by actually campaigning against it in 2007.

The Federal Reserve System, as Rothbard makes crystal clear, was the culmination of efforts that continued throughout the nineteenth century to centralize banking.

> By the 1890s, the leading Wall Street bankers were becoming disgruntled with their own creation, the National Banking System. ... [W]hile the banking system was partially centralized under their leadership, it was not centralized enough.

As he describes the movement to cartelize banking, Rothbard introduces a dominant theme in his interpretation of twentieth-century American history: the struggle of competing groups of bankers for power.

> From the 1890s until World War II, much of American political history ... can be interpreted not so much as "Democrat" versus "Republican" but as the interaction or conflict between the Morgans and their allies on the one hand, and the Rockefeller-Harriman-Kuhn, Loeb alliance on the other.

In the agitation to establish the Fed, the House of Morgan led the way; and Rothbard stresses the importance of the conference held at Jekyll Island, Georgia, in November, 1910, under Morgan control. The entire section of his book *The Case Against the Fed* that deals with the origin of the Fed shows Rothbard's incredibly detailed historical knowledge. Though he was too modest to do so, he could had he wished have echoed the boast of Fustel de Coulanges: "It is not I who speak, but history who speaks through me." Rothbard brings the historical section of the book to a close with a discussion of the Fed's early years in which the Governor of the New York Fed, Benjamin Strong, guaranteed Morgan control. Only with the coming of the New Deal were the Morgan interests relegated to a lesser role, as the Rockefellers assumed leadership of the Eastern Establishment. Rothbard draws attention to the research of Thomas Ferguson, who has interpreted the New Deal as an anti-Morgan coup.

The Fed was supposed to provide stability to the financial sector and the economy at large. We are supposed to believe it has been a wonderful success. A glance at the headlines over the past five years renders an unkind verdict on this rarely examined assumption.

In 2012 we observed another important centenary — the 100-year anniversary of the publication of Ludwig von Mises's pathbreaking book, *The Theory of Money and Credit*, written when the great economist was just 31. The end of an era was approaching as that book reached the public. A century of sound money, albeit with exceptions here and there, was drawing to a close. It had likewise been a century of peace, or at least without a continent-wide war, since the Congress of Vienna. Both of these happy trends came to an abrupt end for the same reason: the outbreak in 1914 of World War I, the great cataclysm of Western civilization.

It was as though Mises had one eye to the past, speaking of the merits of a monetary system which — while not perfectly laissez-faire — had served the world so well for so long, and another eye to the future, as he warned of the consequences of tampering with or abandoning that system. Mises carefully dismantled the inflationist doctrines that were to ravage much of the world during the twentieth century.

That book covered the whole expanse of monetary theory, including money and its origins, interest rates, time preference, banking, credit, inflation, deflation, exchange rates, and business cycles.

Most important for our topic here was Mises's warning to the world's monetary authorities not to suppress the market rate of interest in the name of creating prosperity. The failure to heed Mises's advice, indeed the full-fledged ignorance or outright defiance of that advice, is the monetary story of the twentieth century.

The single most arresting economic event of the Fed's century was surely the Great Depression. This was supposed to have discredited laissez-faire and the free economy for good. Wild speculation was said to have created a stock market bubble, and the bust in 1929 was what the unregulated market had allegedly wrought. Other critics said the problem had been the free market's unfair distribution of wealth: the impoverished masses simply couldn't afford to buy what the stores had for sale. In later years, even so-called free-marketeers would blame the Depression on too little intervention into the market by the Federal Reserve. (With friends like these, who needs enemies?)

Ludwig von Mises offered a different explanation, as did F.A. Hayek, Lionel Robbins, and other scholars working in the Austrian tradition in those days. Murray N. Rothbard, in turn, would devote his 1963 book *America's Great Depression* to an Austrian analysis of this misunderstood episode.

The study of business cycles differs from the study of economic hard times. Economic conditions can be poor because of war, a natural disaster, or some other calamity that disrupts the normal functioning of the market. Business cycle research is not interested in those kinds of conditions. It seeks to understand economic boom and bust when none of these obvious factors are present.

Mises referred to his own approach as the Circulation Credit theory of the business cycle. For our purposes, we can describe it in brief.

On the free market, when people increase their saving, that increased saving has two important consequences. First, it lowers interest rates. These lower interest rates, in turn, make it possible for entrepreneurs to pursue a range of long-term investment projects profitably, thanks to the lower cost of financing. Second, the act of saving and thus abstaining from spending on consumer goods, releases resources that these entrepreneurs can use to complete their new projects. If consumer-goods industries no longer need quite so many resources, since (as we stipulated at the start) people are buying fewer consumer goods, those released resources provide the physical wherewithal to carry out the long-term production projects that the lower interest rates encouraged entrepreneurs to initiate.

Note that it is decisions and actions by the public that provide the means for this capital expansion. "If the public does not provide these means," Mises explains, "they cannot be conjured up by the magic of banking tricks."

But "banking tricks" are precisely how the Fed tries to stimulate the economy. The Fed lowers interest rates artificially, without an increase in saving on the part of the public, and without a corresponding release of resources. The public has not made available the additional means of production necessary to make the array of long-term production projects profitable. The boom will therefore be abortive, and the bust becomes inevitable.

In short, interest rates on a free market reflect people's willingness to abstain from immediate consumption and thereby make resources available for business expansion. They give the entrepreneur an idea of how far and in what ways he may expand. Market interest rates help entrepreneurs distinguish between projects that are appropriate to the current state of resource availability, and projects that are not, projects that the public is willing to sustain by its saving and projects that they are not.

The central bank confuses this process when it intervenes in the market to lower interest rates. As Mises put it:

> The policy of artificially lowering the rate of interest below its potential market height seduces the entrepreneurs to embark upon certain projects of which the public does not approve. In the market economy, each member of society has his share in determining the amount of additional investment. There is no means of fooling the public all of the time by tampering with the rate of interest. Sooner or later, the public's disapproval of a policy of over-expansion takes effect. Then the airy structure of the artificial prosperity collapses.

None of these cycles will be exactly like any other. Roger Garrison says the artificial boom will tend to latch on to and distort whatever the big thing at the time happens to be — tech stocks in the 1990s, for example, and housing in the most recent boom.

With this theoretical apparatus as a guide, Mises became convinced as the 1920s wore on that the seeds of a bust were being sown. This was not a fashionable position. Irving Fisher, a godfather of modern neoclassical economics and the man Milton Friedman called the greatest American economist, could see nothing but continued growth and prosperity in his own survey of economic conditions at the time. In fact, Fisher's predictions in the late 1920s, even in the very midst of the crash, are downright embarrassing.

On September 5, 1929, Fisher wrote: "There may be a recession in stock prices, but not anything in the nature of a crash ... the possibility of which I fail to see."

In mid-October, Fisher said stocks had reached a "permanently high plateau." He expected "to see the stock market a good deal higher than it is today within a few months." He did "not feel that there will soon, if ever, be a fifty- or sixty-point break below present levels."

On October 22, Fisher was speaking of "a mild bull market that will gain momentum next year." With the stock market crashing and values plummeting all around him — with declines far more severe than Fisher had been prepared to admit were even conceivable — Fisher on November 3 insisted that stock prices were "absurdly low." But they would go much lower, ultimately losing 90 percent of their peak value.

What had gone so horribly wrong? Fisher and his colleagues had been blinded by their assumptions. They had been looking at the "price level" and at economic growth figures to determine the health of the economy. They concluded that the 1920s were a period of solid, sustainable economic progress, and were taken completely by surprise by the onset and persistence of the Depression.

Mises, on the other hand, was not fooled by the 1920s. For Mises and the Austrians, crude aggregates of the kind Fisher consulted were not suitable for ascertaining the condition of the economy. To the contrary, these macro-level measurements concealed the economy-wide micro-level maladjustments that resulted from the artificial credit expansion. The misdirection of resources into unsustainable projects, and the expansion or creation of stages of production that the economy cannot sustain, do not show up in national income accounting figures. What matters is that interest rates were pushed lower than they would otherwise have been, thereby leading the economy into an unsustainable configuration that had to be reversed in a bust.

Thus Mises wrote in 1928:

> It is clear that the crisis must come sooner or later. It is also clear that the crisis must always be caused, primarily and directly, by the change in the conduct of the banks. If we speak of error on the part of the banks, however, we must point to the wrong they do in encouraging the upswing. The fault lies, not with the policy of raising the interest rate, but only with the fact that it was raised too late.

Once the crisis hit, Mises showed how his theory of business cycles accounted for what was happening. If people could understand how the crash had come about, Mises hoped, they would be less likely to exacerbate the problem with counterproductive government policy.

"The Causes of the Economic Crisis" was the title of an address Ludwig von Mises delivered in late February 1931 to a group of German industrialists. It was unknown to English-speaking audiences until 1978, when it was published as a chapter in a collection of Mises's essays called *On the Manipulation of Money and Credit*. The Mises Institute published a new edition of these essays in 2006 under the title *The Causes of the Economic Crisis : And Other Essays Before and After the Great Depression*.

In that essay Mises was characteristically blunt in describing the causes of the Great Depression, as well as in his warnings that such crises would recur as long as the authorities continued to pursue the same destructive courses of action.

> The crisis from which we are now suffering is ... the outcome of a credit expansion. The present crisis is the unavoidable sequel to a boom. Such a crisis necessarily follows every boom generated by the attempt to reduce the "natural rate of interest" through increasing the fiduciary media [in other words, through creating credit out of thin air].

Murray Rothbard has explained how and why the Fed undertook this credit expansion. Benjamin Strong, the Governor of the New York Federal Reserve Bank, was by far the most influential figure in the entire Federal Reserve system from its inception until his death in 1928. He entered into close association with Montagu Norman, Governor of the Bank of England. Both men had enlisted in the Morgan camp:

While the close personal relations between Strong and Norman were of course highly important for the collaboration that formed the international monetary world of the 1920s, it should not be overlooked that both were intimately bound to the House of Morgan.

At Norman's behest, Strong inflated the U.S. monetary supply, in order to enable Britain to maintain in operation the gold-exchange standard. By doing so, Rothbard claims, Strong bears heavy responsibility for the onset of the 1929 stock market crash and the ensuing depression.

The United States inflated its money and credit in order to prevent inflationary Britain from losing gold to the United States, a loss which would endanger the new, jerry-built "gold standard" structure. The result, however, was eventual collapse of money and credit in the U.S. and abroad, and a worldwide depression. Benjamin Strong was the Morgans' architect of a disastrous policy of inflationary boom that led inevitably to bust.

Rothbard goes even further in his assault on Federal Reserve inflationism. Contrary to Milton Friedman, the Federal Reserve did not follow a contractionist policy once the depression began. Rothbard assails

the spuriousness of the monetarist legend that the Federal Reserve was responsible for the great contraction of money from 1929 to 1933. On the contrary, the Fed and the administration tried their best to inflate, efforts foiled by the good sense, and by the increasing mistrust of the banking system, of the American people.

The crisis whose wreckage we see all around us right now, a crisis that began in 2008, originated from the same interventions Mises warned against a century ago. Mises would not have been surprised by the Panic of 2008. In 1931 he warned of a recurrence of boom-bust cycles if the policy of artificially low interest rates was not abandoned:

The appearance of periodically recurring economic crises is the necessary consequence of repeatedly renewed attempts to reduce the "natural" rates of interest on the market by means of banking policy. The crises will never disappear so long as men have not learned to avoid such pump-priming, because an artificially stimulated boom must inevitably lead to crisis and depression. ...

All attempts to emerge from the crisis by new interventionist measures are completely misguided. There is only one way out of the crisis. ...

Give up the pursuit of policies which seek to establish interest rates, wage rates, and commodity prices different from those the market indicates.

In the 1920s as now, fashionable opinion could see no major crisis coming. Then as now, the public was assured that the experts at the Fed were smoothing out economic fluctuations and deserved credit for bringing about unprecedented prosperity. And then as now, when the bust came, the free market took the blame for what the Federal Reserve had caused.

Let's look at the crisis of 2008, applying also another vital insight of Mises. Ludwig von Mises had a theory about interventionism. It doesn't accomplish its stated ends. Instead it distorts the market. That distortion cries out for a fix. The fix can consist in pulling back and freeing the market or taking further steps toward intervention. The State nearly always chooses the latter course, unless forced to do otherwise. The result is more distortion, leading eventually, by small steps, toward ever more nationalization and its attendant stagnation and bankruptcy.

When you think about the Fannie Mae-Freddie Mac crisis, you must remember Mises's theory of intervention. Reporters will not, but you must, provided you want to understand what is going on. President Bush considered a fateful step in a 60-year-old problem: the nationalization of these mortgage companies. He wanted to guarantee the $5 trillion (that's trillion with a "t") in debt owned by these companies. Another option would be to put these monstrosities under "conservatorship," which means that you and I will pay for their losses directly.

Either way, it turns out that there is no magic way to put every American citizen, regardless of financial means or credit history, in a 3,000 square foot home. Someone, somewhere, sometime has to pay. No matter what rescue plan they are able to cobble together, that someone is you.

The heck of it is that any option would be devastating to the already-suffering housing market. The reason this sector was so wildly inflated is that banks knew that Fannie and Freddie were capable of buying any mortgage debt created by the banking industry. For these companies to be nationalized would effectively end their capacity to do this on a market basis. That means banks would suddenly have to act responsibly.

Now, you might say, if that's true, the real blame is with the individual bankers that had been making irresponsible loans under the condition that these government-sponsored enterprises would absorb them. But that's not right. Put yourself in the shoes of a banker over the last 20 years. You have competitors. You have a bottom line. If you don't extend these loans, you come off as a fool. Your competition eats your breakfast. To stay ahead of market trends means that you have to play the game, even though you know it is rigged.

Place the blame not only on the banks, but also on the institutions that are siphoning off their liabilities for irresponsible behavior, and that would be Freddie and Fannie. And who created these? Travel back in time to the New Deal

They were created by FDR in 1938 to fund mortgages insured by the Federal Home Administration. They were used by every president as a means to achieve this peculiar American value that every last person must own a home, no matter what. So they were given the legal permission to purchase private mortgages and make them part of their portfolios. Still later, under LBJ and Nixon, they became public companies and sold stock. People called this privatization, but that isn't quite right. They had access to a guaranteed line of credit creation with the US Treasury. They had lower borrowing costs than any private-sector equivalent.

Government-sponsored enterprises are not subject to market discipline like regular private sector companies. Their securities are listed as government securities, so their risk premiums were not dictated by the free market. They could leverage themselves at 50-, 75-, 100-1, pyramiding debt on a tiny foundation of equity. The financial markets have long believed that the GSEs would be bailed out no matter what. And so this put them in a completely different position from a company like Enron, which the markets watched closely. What's causing the current panic is that the markets have wised up and started evaluating these institutions by market standards. Freddie and Fannie have collapsing market prices, and their bonds are carrying ever-higher risk premiums.

In other words, we are not talking about market failure. If you have a housetop you can shout that from, please do so, because the press and the government are going to make every effort to blame private borrowers and lenders for this calamity. But the origin of both these outfits is with federal legislation. They are not market entities. They have long been guaranteed by you and me. No, they have not been socialist entities either because they are privately owned. They occupy a third status for which there is a name: fascism. Really, that's what we are talking about: the inexorable tendency of financial fascism to mutate into full-scale financial socialism and therefore bankruptcy.

Mr. Bush might have prevented this meltdown by curbing the privileges of Freddie and Fannie long ago. But no, he had another plan, one which was assisted by the Republican think tanks in Washington (the curious can Google it up). The idea was a new slogan called the "ownership society."

Sounds nice, doesn't it? Sounds like free enterprise. But if you think about it, there is nothing particularly free market about the demand that everyone should own anything in particular. The idea of free markets is that your rights to own justly are not to be infringed upon by public or private criminals. The suggestion that everyone should own some particular thing, by whatever means, can only be funded through financial socialism or mass theft. The claim on the part of a government that it will create an "ownership society" can prove to be highly dangerous.

As for the future, Mises's theory that the government will always favor more government seems wholly sound. Here is John McCain: "Those institutions, Fannie and Freddie, have been responsible for millions of Americans to be able to own their own homes, and they will not fail, we will not allow them to fail ... we will do what's necessary to make sure that they continue that function." Not a single Democrat disagrees.

As with the S&L fiasco from years ago, the case of the housing bust followed by the trillions in taxpayer liabilities for the disaster will again be cited as a case of "the shock doctrine" and "disaster capitalism" in which the elites make fantastic amounts of money at the expense of the little guy. The critique will be mostly solid but for the one most important point: this kind of fiasco would not happen in a free market. It happens because government, through credit creation and guarantees, makes it possible.

Look down the road a bit here. What happens when banks won't lend for houses anymore? What will government do then? We might as well prepare for a future in which applying for a housing loan will have similar features to getting an SBA loan. This is where we are headed.

Government intervention is like a vial of mutating poison in the water supply. We can get by for a long time and no one seems really worse off. One day we wake up and everyone is desperately ill, and blaming not the poison but the water itself. So it is with the housing crisis. Lenders are being blamed for the entire fiasco, and capitalism is going to be subjected to a beating as usual, since Freddie and Fannie are traded in public markets. But the fact remains that there is only one reason that this went on as long as it did and became as bad as it is. It was that vial of government poison.

It is fitting that a century of the Federal Reserve should come to an end at a moment of economic crisis and uncertainty, with the central bank's leadership confused and in disarray after the economy's failure to respond to unprecedented doses of monetary intervention. The century of the Fed has been a century of depression, recession, inflation, financial bubbles, and unsound banking, and its legacy is the precipice on which our economy now precariously rests.

5

AMERICAN FASCISM

EVERYONE KNOWS THAT THE term fascist is a pejorative, often used to describe any political position a speaker doesn't like. There isn't anyone around who is willing to stand up and say: "I'm a fascist; I think fascism is a great social and economic system."

But I submit that if they were honest, the vast majority of politicians, intellectuals, and political activists would have to say just that.

Fascism is the system of government that cartelizes the private sector, centrally plans the economy to subsidize producers, exalts the police State as the source of order, denies fundamental rights and liberties to individuals, and makes the executive State the unlimited master of society.

This describes mainstream politics in America today. And not just in America. It's true in Europe, too. It is so much part of the mainstream that it is hardly noticed any more.

It is true that fascism has no overarching theoretical apparatus. There is no grand theorist like Marx. That makes it no less real and distinct as a social, economic, and political system. Fascism also thrives as a distinct style of social and economic management. And it is as much or more of a threat to civilization than full-blown socialism.

This is because its traits are so much a part of life — and have been for so long — that they are nearly invisible to us.

If fascism is invisible to us, it is truly the silent killer. It fastens a huge, violent, lumbering State on the free market that drains its capital and productivity like a deadly parasite on a host. This is why the fascist State has been called the Vampire Economy. It sucks the economic life out of a nation and brings about a slow death of a once thriving economy.

Let me just provide an example. After the first sets of data were made public from the 2010 US Census, newspaper headlines were concerned about the huge increase in the poverty rate. It is the largest increase in 20 years, and now up to 15 percent.

But most people hear this and dismiss it, probably for good reason. The poor in this country are not poor by any historical standard. They have cell phones, cable TV, cars, lots of food, and plenty of disposable income. What's more, there is no such thing as a fixed class called the poor. People come and go, depending on age and life circumstances. Plus, in American politics, when you hear kvetching about the poor, everyone knows what you're supposed to do: hand the government your wallet.

Buried in the US Census report is another fact that has much more profound significance. It concerns median household income in real terms.

What the data have revealed is devastating. Since 1999, median household income has fallen 7.1 percent. Since 1989, median family income is largely flat. And since 1973 and the end of the gold standard, it has hardly risen at all. The great wealth generating machine that was once America is failing.

No longer can one generation expect to live a better life than the previous one. The fascist economic model has killed what was once called the American dream. And the truth is, of course, even worse than the statistic reveals. You have to consider how many incomes exist within a single household to make up the total income. After World War II, the single-income family became the norm. Then the money was destroyed and American savings were wiped out and the capital base of the economy was devastated.

It was at this point that households began to struggle to stay above water. The year 1985 was the turning point. This was the year that it became more common than not for a household to have two incomes rather than one. Mothers entered the workforce to keep family income floating.

The intellectuals cheered this trend, as if it represented liberation, shouting hosannas that all women everywhere are now added to the tax rolls as valuable contributors to the State's coffers. The real cause is the rise of fiat money that depreciated the currency, robbed savings, and shoved people into the workforce as taxpayers.

This story is not told in the data alone. You have to look at the demographics to discover it.

This huge demographic shift essentially bought the American household another 20 years of seeming prosperity, though it is hard to call it that since there was no longer any choice about the matter. If you wanted to keep living the dream, the household could no longer get by on a single income.

But this huge shift was merely an escape hatch. It bought 20 years of slight increases before the income trend flattened again. Over the last decade we are back to falling. Today median family income is only slightly above where it was when Nixon wrecked the dollar, put on price and wage controls, created the EPA, and the whole apparatus of the parasitic welfare-warfare State came to be entrenched and made universal.

Yes, this is fascism, and we are paying the price. The dream is being destroyed.

The talk in Washington about reform, whether from Democrats or Republicans, is like a bad joke. They talk of small changes, small cuts, commissions they will establish, curbs they will make in ten years. It is all white noise. None of this will fix the problem. Not even close.

The problem is more fundamental. It is the quality of the money. It is the very existence of 10,000 regulatory agencies. It is the whole assumption that you have to pay the State for the privilege to work. It is the presumption that the government must manage every aspect of the capitalist economic order. In short, it is the total State that is the problem, and the suffering and decline will continue so long as the total State exists.

To be sure, the last time people worried about fascism was during the Second World War. We were said to be fighting this evil system abroad.

The US defeated fascist governments but the philosophy of governance that it represents was not defeated. Very quickly following that war, another one began. This was the Cold War that pitted capitalism against communism. Socialism in this case was considered to be a soft form of communism, tolerable and even praiseworthy insofar as it was linked with democracy, which is the system that legalizes and legitimizes an ongoing pillaging of the population.

In the meantime, almost everyone has forgotten that there are many other colors of socialism, not all of them obviously left wing. Fascism is one of these colors.

There can be no question of its origins. It is tied up with the history of post-World War I Italian politics. In 1922, Benito Mussolini came to power and established fascism as his philosophy. Mussolini had been a member of the socialist party.

All the biggest and most important players within the fascist movement came from the socialists. It was a threat to the socialists because it was the most appealing political vehicle for the real-world application of the socialist impulse. Socialists crossed over to join the fascists en masse.

This is also why Mussolini himself enjoyed such good press for more than ten years after his rule began. He was celebrated by the *New York Times* in article after article. He was heralded in scholarly collections as an exemplar of the type of leader we need in an age of the planned society. Puff pieces on this blowhard were very common in US journalism all through the late 1920s and the mid-1930s.

Remember that in this same period, the American left went through a huge shift. In the teens and 1920s, the American left had a very praiseworthy anti-corporatist impulse. The left generally opposed war, the state-run penal system, alcohol prohibition, and all violations of civil liberties. It was no friend of capitalism but neither was it a friend of the corporate State of the sort that FDR forged during the New Deal.

In 1933 and 1934, the American left had to make a choice. Would they embrace the corporatism and regimentation of the New Deal or take a principled stand on their old liberal values? In other words, would they accept fascism as a halfway house to their socialist utopia? A gigantic battle ensued in this period, and there was a clear winner. The New

Deal made an offer the left could not refuse. And it was a small step to go from the embrace of the fascistic planned economy to the celebration of the warfare State that concluded the New Deal period.

This was merely a repeat of the same course of events in Italy a decade earlier. In Italy too, the left realized that their anti-capitalistic agenda could best be achieved within the framework of the authoritarian, planning State. Of course our friend John Maynard Keynes played a critical role in providing a pseudo-scientific rationale for joining opposition to old-world laissez faire to a new appreciation of the planned society. Recall that Keynes was not a socialist of the old school.

In his preface to the German edition of *The General Theory*, dated September 7, 1936, Keynes indicated that the ideas of his book could more readily be carried out under an authoritarian regime:

> Nevertheless the theory of output as a whole, which is what the following book purports to provide, is more easily adapted to the conditions of a totalitarian state, than is the theory of the production and distribution of a given output under conditions of free competition and a large measure of laissez-faire.

As Donald Moggridge points out, the published German version (but not Keynes's draft) also said,

> Although I have thus worked it [Keynes's theory] out having the conditions in the Anglo-Saxon countries in view — where a great deal of laissez-faire still prevails — it yet remains applicable to situations in which national leadership is more pronounced.

Keynes's comments did not come out of the blue. In the 1930s, Hitler was widely viewed as just another protectionist central planner who recognized the supposed failure of the free market and the need for nationally guided economic development. Proto-Keynesian socialist economist Joan Robinson wrote that "Hitler found a cure against unemployment before Keynes was finished explaining it."

The most definitive study on fascism written in these years was *As We Go Marching* by John T. Flynn. Flynn was a journalist and scholar of a liberal spirit who had written a number of best-selling books in the 1920s. He could probably be put in the progressive camp in the 1920s. It was the New Deal that changed him. His colleagues all followed FDR into fascism, while Flynn himself kept the old faith. That meant that he fought FDR every step of the way, and not only his domestic plans. Flynn was a leader of the America First movement that saw FDR's drive to war as nothing but an extension of the New Deal, which it certainly was.

But because Flynn was part of what Murray Rothbard later dubbed the Old Right — Flynn came to oppose both the welfare State and the warfare State — his name went down the Orwellian memory hole after the war, during the heyday of CIA conservatism.

As We Go Marching came out in 1944, just at the tail end of the war, and right in the midst of wartime economic controls the world over. It is a wonder that it ever got past the censors. It is a full-scale study of fascist theory and practice, and Flynn saw precisely where fascism ends: in militarism and war as the fulfillment of the stimulus-spending agenda. When you run out of everything else to spend money on, you can always depend on nationalist fervor to back more military spending.

In reviewing the history of the rise of fascism, Flynn wrote:

> One of the most baffling phenomena of fascism is the almost incredible collaboration between men of the extreme Right and the extreme Left in its creation. The explanation lies at this point. Both Right and Left joined in this urge for regulation. The motives, the arguments, and the forms of expression were different but all drove in the same direction. And this was that the economic system must be controlled in its essential functions and this control must be exercised by the producing groups.

Flynn writes that the right and the left disagreed on precisely who fits the bill as the producer group. The left tends to celebrate laborers as producers. The right tends to favor business owners as producers. The political compromise — and it still goes on today — was to cartelize both.

Government under fascism becomes the cartelization device for both workers and the private owners of capital. Competition between workers and between businesses is regarded as wasteful and pointless; the political elites decide that the members of these groups need to get together and cooperate under government supervision to build a mighty nation.

The fascists have always been obsessed with the idea of national greatness. To them, this does not consist in a nation of people who are growing more prosperous, living ever better and longer lives. No, national greatness occurs when the State embarks on building huge monuments, undertaking nationwide transportation systems, carving Mount Rushmore, or digging the Panama Canal.

In other words, national greatness is not the same thing as your greatness or your family's greatness or your company's or profession's greatness. On the contrary. You have to be taxed, your money's value has to be depreciated, your privacy invaded, and your well being diminished in order to achieve it. In this view, the government has to make us great.

Tragically, such a program has a far greater chance of political success than old-fashioned socialism. Fascism doesn't nationalize private property as socialism does. That means that the economy doesn't collapse right away. Nor does fascism push to equalize incomes. There is no talk of the abolition of marriage or the nationalization of children.

Religion is not abolished but used as a tool of political manipulation. The fascist State was far more politically astute in this respect than communism. It wove together religion and statism into one package, encouraging a worship of God provided that the State operates as the intermediary.

Under fascism, society as we know it is left intact, though everything is lorded over by a mighty State apparatus. Whereas traditional socialist teaching fostered a globalist perspective, fascism was explicitly nationalist. It embraced and exalted the idea of the nation-state.

As for the bourgeoisie, fascism doesn't seek their expropriation. Instead, the middle class gets what it wants in the form of social insurance, medical benefits, and heavy doses of national pride.

It is for all these reasons that fascism takes on a right-wing cast. It doesn't attack fundamental bourgeois values. It draws on them to garner support for a democratically backed all-round national regimentation of economic control, censorship, cartelization, political intolerance, geographic expansion, executive control, the police State, and militarism.

For my part, I have no problem referring to the fascist program as a right-wing theory, even if it does fulfill aspects of the left-wing dream. The crucial matter here concerns its appeal to the public and to the demographic groups that are normally drawn to right-wing politics.

If you think about it, right-wing statism is of a different color, cast, and tone from left-wing statism. Each is designed to appeal to a different set of voters with different interests and values.

These divisions, however, are not strict, and we've already seen how a left-wing socialist program can adapt itself and become a right-wing fascist program with very little substantive change other than its marketing program.

The Eight Marks of Fascist Policy

John T. Flynn, like other members of the Old Right, was disgusted by the irony that what he saw, most everyone else chose to ignore. In the fight against authoritarian regimes abroad, he noted, the US had adopted those forms of government at home, complete with price controls, rationing, censorship, executive dictatorship, and even concentration camps for whole groups considered to be unreliable in their loyalties to the State.

After reviewing this long history, Flynn proceeds to sum up with a list of eight points he considers to be the main marks of the fascist State.

As I present them, I will also offer comments on the modern American central State.

Point 1. The government is totalitarian because it acknowledges no restraint upon its powers

This is a very telling mark. It suggests that the US political system can be described as totalitarian. This is a shocking remark that most people would reject. But they can reject this characterization so long as they happen not to be directly ensnared in the State's web. If they become so, they will quickly discover that there are indeed no limits to what the State can do. This can happen boarding a flight, driving around in your home town, or having your business run afoul of some government agency. In the end, you must obey or be caged like an animal or killed. In this way, no matter how much you may believe that you are free, all of us today are but one step away from Guantanamo.

As recently as the 1990s, I can recall that there were moments when Clinton seemed to suggest that there were some things that his administration could not do. Today I'm not so sure that I can recall any government official pleading the constraints of law or the constraints of reality to what can and cannot be done. No aspect of life is untouched by government intervention, and often it takes forms we do not readily see. All of health care is regulated, but so is every bit of our food, transportation, clothing, household products, and even private relationships.

Mussolini himself put his principle this way: "All within the State, nothing outside the State, nothing against the State." He also said: "The keystone of the Fascist doctrine is its conception of the State, of its essence, its functions, and its aims. For Fascism the State is absolute, individuals and groups relative."

I submit to you that this is the prevailing ideology in the United States today. This nation conceived in liberty has been kidnapped by the fascist State.

POINT 2. GOVERNMENT IS A DE FACTO DICTATORSHIP BASED ON THE LEADERSHIP PRINCIPLE

I wouldn't say that we truly have a dictatorship of one man in this country, but we do have a form of dictatorship of one sector of government over the entire country. The executive branch has spread so dramatically over the last century that it has become a joke to speak of checks and balances. What the kids learn in civics class has nothing to do with reality.

The executive State is the State as we know it, all flowing from the White House down. The role of the courts is to enforce the will of the executive. The role of the legislature is to ratify the policy of the executive.

Further, this executive is not really about the person who seems to be in charge. The president is only the veneer, and the elections are only the tribal rituals we undergo to confer some legitimacy on the institution. In reality, the nation-state lives and thrives outside any "democratic mandate." Here we find the power to regulate all aspects of life and the wicked power to create the money necessary to fund this executive rule.

As for the leadership principle, there is no greater lie in American public life than the propaganda we hear every four years about how the new president/messiah is going to usher in the great dispensation of peace, equality, liberty, and global human happiness. The idea here is that the whole of society is really shaped and controlled by a single will — a point that requires a leap of faith so vast that you have to disregard everything you know about reality to believe it.

And yet people do. The hope for a messiah reached a fevered pitch with Obama's election. The civic religion was in full-scale worship mode — of the greatest human who ever lived or ever shall live. It was a despicable display.

Another lie that the American people believe is that presidential elections bring about regime change. This is sheer nonsense. The Obama State is the Bush State; the Bush State was the Clinton State; the Clinton State was the Bush State; the Bush State was the Reagan State. We can trace this back and back in time and see overlapping appointments, bureaucrats, technicians, diplomats, Fed officials, financial elites, and so on. Rotation in office occurs not because of elections but because of mortality.

POINT 3. GOVERNMENT ADMINISTERS A CAPITALIST SYSTEM WITH AN IMMENSE BUREAUCRACY

The reality of bureaucratic administration has been with us at least since the New Deal, which was modeled on the planning bureaucracy that lived in World War I. The planned economy — whether in Mussolini's time or ours — requires bureaucracy. Bureaucracy is the heart, lungs, and veins of the planning State. And yet to regulate an economy as thoroughly as this one is today is to kill prosperity with a billion tiny cuts.

This doesn't necessarily mean economic contraction, at least right away. But it definitely means killing off growth that would have otherwise occurred in a free market.

So where is our growth? Where is the peace dividend that was supposed to come after the end of the Cold War? Where are the fruits of the amazing gains in efficiency that technology has afforded? It has been eaten by the bureaucracy that manages our every move on this earth. The voracious and insatiable monster here is called the Federal Code that calls on thousands of agencies to exercise the police power to prevent us from living free lives.

It is as Bastiat said: The real cost of the State is the prosperity we do not see, the jobs that don't exist, the technologies to which we do not have access, the businesses that do not come into existence, and the bright future that is stolen from us. The State has looted us just as surely as a robber who enters our home at night and steals all that we love.

POINT 4. PRODUCERS ARE ORGANIZED INTO CARTELS IN THE WAY OF SYNDICALISM

Syndicalist is not usually how we think of how our current economic structure. But remember that syndicalism means economic control by the producers. Capitalism is different. It places by virtue of market structures all control in the hands of the consumers. The only question for syndicalists, then, is which producers are going to enjoy political privilege. It might be the workers but it can also be the largest corporations.

In the case of the US, in recent years, we've seen giant banks, pharmaceutical firms, insurers, car companies, Wall Street banks and brokerage houses, and quasi-private mortgage companies enjoying vast privileges at our expense. They have all joined with the State in living a parasitical existence at our expense.

This is also an expression of the syndicalist idea, and it has cost the US economy untold trillions and sustained an economic depression by preventing the post-boom adjustment that markets would otherwise dictate. The government has tightened its syndicalist grip in the name of stimulus.

POINT 5. ECONOMIC PLANNING IS BASED ON THE PRINCIPLE OF AUTARKY

Autarky is the name given to the idea of economic self-sufficiency. Mostly this refers to the economic self-determination of the nation-state. The nation-state must be geographically huge in order to support rapid economic growth for a large and growing population.

This was and is the basis for fascist expansionism. Without expansion, the State dies. This is also the idea behind the strange combination of protectionist pressure today combined with militarism. It is driven in part by the need to control resources. As Mises observes in *Omnipotent Government*,

> There are nations which for lack of adequate resources cannot feed and clothe their population out of domestic resources. These nations cannot aim at autarky, but by embarking upon a policy of conquest. With

them bellicosity and lust of aggression are the outcome of their adherence to the principles of government control of business. This was the case with Germany, Italy, and Japan. They said that they wanted to get a fair share of the earth's resources, thus they aimed at a new distribution of the areas producing raw materials. But these other countries were not empty; their inhabitants were not prepared to consider themselves as an appurtenance of their mines and plantations. They did not long for German or Italian rule. Thus there originated conflicts.

Look at the wars in Iraq, Afghanistan, and Libya. We would be supremely naïve to believe that these wars were not motivated in part by the producer interests of the oil industry. It is true of the American empire generally, which supports dollar hegemony.

It is the reason for the planned North American Union.

The goal is national self-sufficiency rather than a world of peaceful trade. Consider, too, the protectionist impulses of the Republican ticket. There is not one single Republican, apart from Ron Paul, who authentically supports free trade in the classical definition.

From ancient Rome to modern-day America, imperialism is a form of statism that the bourgeoisie love. It is for this reason that Bush's post-09/11 push for the global empire was sold as patriotism and love of country rather than for what it was: a looting of liberty and property to benefit the political elites.

POINT 6. GOVERNMENT SUSTAINS ECONOMIC LIFE THROUGH SPENDING AND BORROWING

This point requires no elaboration because it is no longer hidden. There was stimulus 1 and stimulus 2, both of which are so discredited that stimulus 3 will have to adopt a new name. Let's call it the American Jobs Act.

With a prime-time speech, Obama argued in favor of this program with some of the most asinine economic analysis I've ever heard. He mused about how is it that people are unemployed at a time when schools, bridges, and infrastructure need repairing. He ordered that supply and demand come together to match up needed work with jobs.

Hello? The schools, bridges, and infrastructure that Obama refers to are all built and maintained by the State. That's why they are falling apart.

And people don't have jobs because the State has made it too expensive to hire them. It's not complicated. To sit around and dream of other scenarios is no different from wishing that water flowed uphill or that rocks would float in the air. It amounts to a denial of reality.

Still, Obama went on, invoking the old fascistic longing for national greatness. "Building a world-class transportation system," he said, "is part of what made us an economic superpower." Then he asked: "We're going to sit back and watch China build newer airports and faster railroads?"

Well, the answer to that question is yes. And you know what? It doesn't hurt a single American for a person in China to travel on a faster railroad than we do. To claim otherwise is an incitement to nationalist hysteria.

As for the rest of this program, Obama promised yet another long list of spending projects. Let's just mention the reality: No government in the history of the world has spent as much, borrowed as much, and created as much fake money as the US. If the US doesn't qualify as a fascist State in this sense, no government ever has.

None of this would be possible but for the role of the Federal Reserve, the great lender to the world. This institution is absolutely critical to US fiscal policy. There is no way that the national debt could increase at a rate of $4 billion per day without this institution.

Under a gold standard, all of this maniacal spending would come to an end. And if US debt were priced on the market with a default premium, we would be looking at a rating far less than A+.

POINT 7. MILITARISM IS A MAINSTAY OF GOVERNMENT SPENDING

Have you ever noticed that the military budget is never seriously discussed in policy debates? The US spends more than most of the rest of the world combined.

And yet to hear our leaders talk, the US is just a tiny commercial republic that wants peace but is constantly under threat from the world. They would have us believe that we all stand naked and vulnerable. The whole thing is a ghastly lie. The US is a global military empire and the main threat to peace around the world today.

To visualize US military spending as compared with other countries is truly shocking. One bar chart you can easily look up shows the US trillion-dollar-plus military budget as a skyscraper surrounded by tiny huts. As for the next highest spender, China spends 1/10th as much as the US.

Where is the debate about this policy? Where is the discussion? It is not going on. It is just assumed by both parties that it is essential for the US way of life that the US be the most deadly country on the planet, threatening everyone with nuclear extinction unless they obey. This should be considered a fiscal and moral outrage by every civilized person.

This isn't only about the armed services, the military contractors, the CIA death squads. It is also about how police at all levels have taken on military-like postures. This goes for the local police, State police, and even the crossing guards in our communities. The commissar mentality, the trigger-happy thuggishness, has become the norm throughout the whole of society.

If you want to witness outrages, it is not hard. Try coming into this country from Canada or Mexico. See the bullet-proof-vest wearing, heavily armed, jackbooted thugs running dogs up and down car lanes, searching people randomly, harassing innocents, asking rude and intrusive questions.

You get the strong impression that you are entering a police State. That impression would be correct.

Yet for the man on the street, the answer to all social problems seems to be more jails, longer terms, more enforcement, more arbitrary power, more crackdowns, more capital punishments, more authority. Where does all of this end? And will the end come before we realize what has happened to our once-free country?

POINT 8. MILITARY SPENDING HAS IMPERIALIST AIMS

Ronald Reagan used to claim that his military buildup was essential to keeping the peace. The history of US foreign policy just since the 1980s has shown that this is wrong. We've had one war after another, wars waged by the US against non-compliant countries, and the creation of even more client states and colonies.

US military strength has not led to peace, but the opposite. It has caused most people in the world to regard the US as a threat, and it has led to unconscionable wars on many countries. Wars of aggression were defined at Nuremberg as crimes against humanity.

Obama was supposed to end this. He never promised to do so. But his supporters all believed that he would. Instead, he has done the opposite. He has increased troop levels, entrenched wars, and started new ones. In reality, he has presided over a warfare State just as vicious as any in history. The difference this time is that the left is no longer criticizing the US role in the world. In that sense, Obama is the best thing to ever happen to the warmongers and the military-industrial complex.

As for the right in this country, it once opposed this kind of military fascism. But all that changed after the beginning of the Cold War. The right was led into a terrible ideological shift, well documented in Murray Rothbard's neglected masterpiece *The Betrayal of the American Right*. In the name of stopping communism, the right came to follow ex-CIA agent Bill Buckley's endorsement of a totalitarian bureaucracy at home to fight wars all over the world.

Buckley stated this premise early in his career: "[I]n his January 1952 essay in *Commonweal* Buckley wrote that given the 'thus-far invincible aggressiveness of the Soviet Union ... we have got to accept Big Government for the duration.'" Buckley here expressed no mere passing thought. Putting into action his belief in a crusade against Communism, he had after graduation from Yale joined the CIA for a brief period from 1950–51.

John T. Flynn, a stalwart of the Old Right, was a fervent anti-communist, but he warned against a military buildup supposedly designed to contain Stalin and his successors. To impose military socialism at home would not help to defeat communism; rather, it would increase militarism, which "was and remains a racket, the oldest in history" to unprecedented levels.

Simple common sense, one would suppose; but Flynn's classic defense of Old Right thinking was not to the liking of the warmongering editor of the newly founded *National Review*. When Flynn submitted an article to *National Review* that warned against militarism and war, Buckley returned it to Flynn writing, "This piece just isn't what I had in mind."

Murray Rothbard, as usual, has the best comment on Buckley's brand of conservatism. The theoreticians of *National Review*:

transformed the Right from a movement that, at least roughly, believed first of all in individual liberty (and its corollaries: civil liberties domestically, and peace and "isolation" in foreign affairs) into a movement that, in fact glorifies total war and the suppression of civil liberty.

At the end of the Cold War, there was a brief reprise when the right in this country remembered its roots in non-interventionism. But this did not last long. George Bush the First rekindled the militarist spirit with the first war on Iraq, and there has been no fundamental questioning of the American empire ever since. Even today, Republicans — except, again, Ron Paul — elicit their biggest applause by whipping up audiences about foreign threats, while never mentioning that the real threat to American well-being exists in the Beltway.

THE FUTURE

I can think of no greater priority today than a serious and effective antifascist alliance. In many ways, one is already forming. It is not a formal alliance. It is made up of those who protest the Fed, those who refuse to go along with mainstream fascist politics, those who seek decentralization, those who demand lower taxes and free trade, those who seek the right to associate with anyone they want and buy and sell on terms of their own choosing, those who insist they can educate their children on their own, the investors and savers who make economic growth possible, those who do not want to be felt up at airports, and those who have become expatriates.

It is also made of the millions of independent entrepreneurs who are discovering that the number one threat to their ability to serve others through the commercial marketplace is the institution that claims to be our biggest benefactor: the government.

How many people fall into this category? It is more than we know. The movement is intellectual. It is political. It is cultural. It is technological. They come from all classes, races, countries, and professions. This is no longer a national movement. It is truly global.

We can no longer predict whether members consider themselves to be left wing, right wing, independent, libertarian, anarchist, or something else. It includes those as diverse as home-schooling parents in the suburbs as well as parents in urban areas whose children are among the

2.3 million people who languish in jail for no good reason in a country with the largest prison population in the world.

And what does this movement want? Nothing more or less than sweet liberty. It does not ask that the liberty be granted or given. It only asks for the liberty that is promised by life itself and would otherwise exist were it not for the leviathan State that robs us, badgers us, jails us, kills us.

This movement is not departing. We are daily surrounded by evidence that it is right and true. Every day, it is more and more obvious that the State contributes absolutely nothing to our well-being, but massively subtracts from it.

Back in the 1930s, and even up through the 1980s, the partisans of the State were overflowing with ideas. They had theories and agendas that had many intellectual backers. They were thrilled and excited about the world they would create. They would end business cycles, bring about social advance, build the middle class, cure disease, bring about universal security, and much more. Fascism believed in itself.

This is no longer true. Fascism has no new ideas, no big projects, and not even its partisans really believe it can accomplish what it sets out to do. The world created by the private sector is so much more useful and beautiful than anything the State has done that the fascists have themselves become demoralized and aware that their agenda has no real intellectual foundation.

It is ever more widely known that statism does not and cannot work. Statism is the great lie. Statism gives us the exact opposite of its promise. It promised security, prosperity, and peace; it has given us fear, poverty, war, and death. If we want a future, it is one that we have to build ourselves. The fascist State will not give it to us; on the contrary, it stands in the way.

It also seems to me that the old-time romance of the classical liberals with the idea of the limited State is gone. It is far more likely today that young people embrace an idea that 50 years ago was thought to be the unthinkable thought: the idea that society is best off without any State at all.

I would mark the rise of anarcho-capitalist theory as the most dramatic intellectual shift in my adult lifetime. Gone is that view of the State as the night watchman that would only guard essential rights, adjudicate disputes, and protect liberty.

This view is woefully naïve. The night watchman is the guy with the guns, the legal right to use aggression, the guy who controls all comings and goings, the guy who is perched on top and sees all things. Who is watching him? Who is limiting his power? No one, and this is precisely why he is the very source of society's greatest ills. No constitution, no election, no social contract will check his power.

Indeed, the night watchman has acquired total power. It is he who would be the total State, which Flynn describes as a government that "possesses the power to enact any law or take any measure that seems proper to it." So long as a government, he says, "is clothed with the power to do anything without any limitation on its powers, it is totalitarian. It has total power."

It is no longer a point that we can ignore. The night watchman must be removed and his powers distributed within and among the whole population, and they should be governed by the same forces that bring us all the blessings the material world affords us.

In the end, this is the choice we face: the total State or total freedom. Which will we choose? If we choose the State, we will continue to sink further and further and eventually lose all that we treasure as a civilization. If we choose freedom, we can harness that remarkable power of human cooperation that will enable us to continue to make a better world.

In the fight against fascism, there is no reason to be despairing but rather to continue to fight with every bit of confidence that the future belongs to us and not to them.

Their world is falling apart. Ours is just being built.

Their world is based on bankrupt ideologies. Ours is rooted in the truth about freedom and reality.

Their world can only look back to the glory days. Ours looks forward to the future we are building for ourselves.

Their world is rooted in the corpse of the nation-state. Our world draws on the energies and creativity of all peoples in the world, united in the great and noble project of creating a prospering civilization through peaceful human cooperation.

It's true that they have the biggest guns. But big guns have not assured permanent victory in Iraq or Afghanistan, or any other place on the planet.

We possess the only weapon that is truly immortal: the right idea. It is this that will lead to victory.

As Mises said:

> In the long run even the most despotic governments with all their brutality and cruelty are no match for ideas. Eventually the ideology that has won the support of the majority will prevail and cut the ground from under the tyrant's feet. Then the oppressed many will rise in rebellion and overthrow their masters.

6

WHY NOT
LIMITED GOVERNMENT?

SO FAR, WE'VE SEEN THAT something is drastically wrong with the American State. The American State is a war state; it makes war both on foreign peoples and on our own people. The War on Drugs and the Patriot Act are only a few examples of what the State is doing to us. The Fed makes sure we have an unstable economy, and American Fascism is firmly locked in place. Things certainly look bad.

But why should we support anarchy? Isn't anarcho-capitalism too risky a policy to adopt? Instead, why not just abandon the war system and return to the non-interventionist foreign policy of the Founding Fathers? In domestic affairs, why not return to a government of strictly limited powers, as Thomas Jefferson wanted?

This program won't work. To begin with, we should be clear that American Fascism wasn't something that FDR imposed on a totally free America. It had deep roots in the policies of Alexander Hamilton, Henry Clay, and Abraham Lincoln.

Tom DiLorenzo helps us to understand this unfortunate part of the American tradition. As he points out in his great book *Hamilton's Curse*, Thomas Jefferson supported the American Revolution in order to promote individual liberty. To secure this end, it was essential that the central government be strictly limited in its powers. America, in the Jeffersonian view, was an alliance of sovereign states, and the adoption of the

Constitution, though it increased the power of the national government, did not fundamentally change this arrangement.

Alexander Hamilton disagreed. He bemoaned the limited powers given to the central government under the Articles of Confederation and continually agitated for a new scheme of authority. At the Constitutional Convention, it became clear how radical were his plans. He favored a permanent president and senate and wanted the federal government to have the power to appoint state governors.

What was behind this radical plan of centralization, fortunately rejected by the majority of the convention? DiLorenzo follows up the brilliant suggestion of Cecilia Kenyon that Hamilton was the "Rousseau of the Right." Rousseau thought that society should be guided by the "general will," but what exactly that concept entailed has perplexed later commentators. It cannot be equated with what the majority of a certain society wishes: it is only when the people's decisions properly reflect the common good, untrammeled by faction, that the general will operates. But if the general will need not result from straightforward voting, how is it to be determined? One answer, for which there is some textual support in Rousseau, is that a wise legislator will guide the people toward what they really want. Those who dissent will "be forced to be free."

This was precisely Hamilton's view. Government, directed by the wise such as himself, would guide the people toward what was good for them. Clinton Rossiter, a Cornell political scientist,

> catalogued how some version of "the general will" appears hundreds of times in Hamilton's speeches, letters, and writings. ... Hamilton more pointedly than any other political thinker of his time, introduced the concept of the "public good" into American thought.

Hamilton did not secure what he wanted at the Convention, and in his contributions to the *Federalist Papers*, he sometimes for purposes of propaganda defended the limited government that he really rejected. But with the onset of the new government in 1789, he by no means abandoned his goal of centralized power. He had been, during the American Revolution, George Washington's military aide; and the new president appointed him secretary of the Treasury. In that capacity, he bombarded Washington with advice on interpreting the Constitution.

The powers of the central government in his view were not confined to those expressly delegated to it — far from it. The national government had also various powers "implied" by its express grants, though the logic of these implications escaped those not enamored of big government. "'Implied powers' are powers that are not actually in the Constitution but that statists like Hamilton wish were there." The government also had "resulting" powers: these were not even present in the Constitution by implication but "resulted" from new situations. If, e.g., the government conquered new territory, it acquired sovereign power over it. "This would be rather the result from the whole mass of the government ... than a consequence of ... powers specially enumerated" (quoting Hamilton).

As if this were not enough, Hamilton did not scruple to interpret the words of the Constitution against their plain sense. Congress was granted the power to pass laws "necessary and proper" for its enumerated powers. To Hamilton, "necessary" meant "convenient"; what was the small matter of the dictionary to stand in the way of the public interest?

In other words, such powers should be made up, even fabricated, on the whims of politicians posing as guardians of the "public good." Hamilton went on to say that any act of government is to be permitted if it is not expressly prohibited by the Constitution, something he forgot to mention in the *Federalist Papers*.

Thus, in his report to Washington on the constitutionality of a national bank, Hamilton held that, since Congress had the power to coin money, and in his opinion a national bank would be helpful for a monetary system, the bank passed the constitutional test. Jefferson disagreed. Regardless of whether Hamilton was right about the desirability of a bank — and Jefferson of course rejected Hamilton's view of the matter — a bank was not "necessary" and hence had no constitutional warrant.

As his opinion on the bank suggests, much of Hamilton's centralizing plans aimed at economic goals. Once more in contrast to Jefferson, he believed that the government should guide the economy. He returned to the mercantilist system famously condemned by Adam Smith in *The Wealth of Nations* (Murray Rothbard has noted that Smith failed completely to repudiate mercantilism; nevertheless, he strongly criticized the main planks of that system).

For Hamilton, economics and politics were tightly bound together. Here DiLorenzo follows Douglass Adair, perhaps the foremost twentieth-century student of the *Federalist Papers*. By tying members of the business elite of the states to the new central government, in large part through their involvement in government debt, the power of the national government would be secured.

> With devious brilliance, Hamilton set out, by a program of class legislation, to unite the propertied interests of the eastern seaboard into a cohesive administration party, while at the same time he attempted to make the executive dominant over the Congress by a lavish use of the spoils system. (quoting Adair)

We have already alluded to two of the components of Hamilton's economic system, a public debt and a national bank. Protective tariffs in his view were also vital. By tariffs, as well as "bounties," the industrial power of the nation could be built up. But why does the growth of industry require the government's help? In Hamilton's famous argument, "infant industries" needed time to establish themselves before they were fit to face the rigors of international competition. DiLorenzo responds that in practice, the infants never reach maturity. The subsidies remain in perpetuity.

Unfortunately, Hamilton was not an aberration. He had many influential followers and successors; and DiLorenzo finds that efforts to centralize economic and political power run through our history, like the proverbial red thread in the ropes of the British navy. One of the foremost of DiLorenzo's long list of villains is John Marshall, the third chief justice and, incidentally, Jefferson's cousin. Marshall was avid to interpret the Constitution in accord with Hamilton's passion for national power. In *McCulloch v. Maryland*, (1819) he upheld the constitutionality of the first Bank of the United States, agreeing with Hamilton on the lax interpretation of "necessary and proper."

As the legal scholar Edwin S. Corwin pointed out, it is "well known" that for his written opinion in this case, Marshall depended on Alexander Hamilton's earlier argument about the constitutionality of the BUS (Bank of the United States), which he had written on February 23, 1791.

In *Fletcher v. Peck* (1810), Marshall set aside state legislation as a violation of a valid contract, even though the "contract" in question was fraudulent. He did so in order to enhance federal supremacy.

Readers of DiLorenzo's earlier books will not be surprised to find Henry Clay on the list of miscreants. All the basic elements of Clay's famous American System came from Hamilton: high tariffs, government promotion of industry, and investment in "internal improvements" such as canals and turnpikes. "Henry Clay, leader of the Whig Party ... would adopt Hamilton's agenda as his own under the rubric of 'The American System,' a slogan that Hamilton himself coined." DiLorenzo points out that these programs made regional strife much worse, since they advanced the interests of the more industrialized Northern states at the expense of the South.

Of course Clay had a follower of his own — Abraham Lincoln, who viewed himself as Clay's disciple. He too favored high tariffs, and his insistence on collecting the "duties and imposts," as he put it in his First Inaugural, made inevitable the War Between the States. Once the war began, Lincoln proceeded to enact as much of the American System as he could, e.g., massive subsidies to railroads and continued high tariffs. To pay for the war and his nationalist economic program, a federal income tax was imposed in 1862.

The Fed and American Fascism just carried further and intensified the trend that Hamilton started.

Well, you might say, even if the statist, fascist tradition goes very far back in American history, can't people reverse it? Can't we return to limited government, as the Constitution mandates?

This solution can't work. It suffers from a fatal flaw. The Constitution creates a government that is the judge of its own powers. The branches of the government, legislative, executive, and judicial, are in theory supposed to check and balance each other. The problem with this is that the Supreme Court, which as the Constitution has developed has become the highest arbiter of constitutional issues, is itself part of the federal government. In a dispute between the federal government and the people, it is unlikely to side against the government.

As Rothbard points out in *The Anatomy of the State*, one major political theorist who recognized — and largely in advance — the glaring loophole in a constitutional limit on government of placing the ultimate interpreting power in the Supreme Court was John C. Calhoun. In his *Disquisition*, Calhoun demonstrated the inherent tendency of the State to break through the limits of such a constitution:

> A written constitution certainly has many and considerable advantages, but it is a great mistake to suppose that the mere insertion of provisions to restrict and limit the power of the government, without investing those for whose protection they are inserted with the means of enforcing their observance will be sufficient to prevent the major and dominant party from abusing its powers. Being the party in possession of the government, they will, from the same constitution of man which makes government necessary to protect society, be in favor of the powers granted by the constitution and opposed to the restrictions intended to limit them. ... The minor or weaker party, on the contrary, would take the opposite direction and regard them [the restrictions] as essential to their protection against the dominant party. ... But where there are no means by which they could compel the major party to observe the restrictions, the only resort left them would be a strict construction of the constitution. ... To this the major party would oppose a liberal construction. ... It would be construction against construction — the one to contract and the other to enlarge the powers of the government to the utmost. But of what possible avail could the strict construction of the minor party be, against the liberal construction of the major, when the one would have all the power of the government to carry its construction into effect and the other be deprived of all means of enforcing its construction? In a contest so unequal, the result would not be doubtful. The party in favor of the restrictions would be overpowered. ... The end of the contest would be the subversion of the constitution ... the restrictions would ultimately be annulled and the government be converted into one of unlimited powers.

"All right," you might say, "we can't rely on an agency within the government to limit the government. We can't trust the government to limit itself. But isn't there a solution to this problem that avoids so radical a step as anarchism? We already know what this is, because we have talked about it in the discussion of the Civil War. Isn't States' Rights the way to go? If a State can nullify an unconstitutional law, and if necessary secede from the Union, won't this be an effective check to the federal government? Unlike our present system a branch of the federal government wouldn't decide how much power the federal government should have."

This would undoubtedly be better than what we have now, but this plan also suffers from an obvious problem. Rothbard diagnoses this problem in a way that has never been surpassed. He also leads us to the true solution.

> In theory, the ensuing constitutional system would assure that the Federal Government check any state invasion of individual rights, while the states would check excessive Federal power over the individual. And yet, while limitations would undoubtedly be more effective than at present, there are many difficulties and problems in the Calhoun solution. If, indeed, a subordinate interest should rightfully have a veto over matters concerning it, then why stop with the states? Why not place veto power in counties, cities, wards? Furthermore, interests are not only sectional, they are also occupational, social, etc. What of bakers or taxi drivers or any other occupation? Should *they* not be permitted a veto power over their own lives? This brings us to the important point that the nullification theory confines its checks to *agencies of government* itself. Let us not forget that federal and state governments, and their respective branches, are still states, are still guided by their own state interests rather than by the interests of the private citizens. What is to prevent the Calhoun system from working in reverse, with states tyrannizing over *their* citizens and only vetoing the federal government when it tries to intervene to *stop* that state tyranny? Or for states to acquiesce in federal tyranny? What is to prevent federal and state governments from forming mutually profitable alliances for the joint exploitation of the citizenry? And even if the private occupational groupings were to be given some form of "functional" representation in government, what is to prevent them from using the State to gain subsidies and other special privileges for themselves or from imposing compulsory cartels on their own members?

> In short, Calhoun does not push his pathbreaking theory on concurrence far enough: he does not push it down to the *individual* himself. If the individual, after all, is the one whose rights are to be protected, then a consistent theory of concurrence would imply veto power by every individual; that is, some form of "unanimity principle." When Calhoun wrote that it should be "impossible to put or to keep it [the government] in action without the concurrent consent of all," he was, perhaps unwittingly, implying just such a conclusion. But such speculation begins to

take us away from our subject, for down this path lie political systems which could hardly be called "States" at all. For one thing, just as the right of nullification for a state logically implies its right of *secession*, so a right of individual nullification would imply the right of any individual to "secede" from the State under which he lives."

In his great work *Liberalism*, Mises also recognized that the logic of secession requires that individuals have a right to secede. The right of self-determination in regard to the question of membership in a state thus means: whenever the inhabitants of a particular territory, whether it be a single village, a whole district, or a series of adjacent districts, make it known, by a freely conducted plebiscite, that they no longer wish to remain united to the state to which they belong at the time, but wish either to form an independent state or to attach themselves to some other state, their wishes are to be respected and complied with. This is the only feasible and effective way of preventing revolutions and civil and international wars.

If it were in any way possible to grant this right of self-determination to every individual person, it would have to be done.

It's hardly surprising that those in control of the State evade Constitutional limits in order to extend their own power. Rulers have always done so, and at least since the time of Machiavelli, ideologists have not been wanting to support their grasp for power and disregard for moral virtue.

The Roman moralists of antiquity, and the Renaissance humanists who followed them, had urged that rulers had to possess a particular set of moral virtues. These were, first, the four cardinal virtues — cardinal from the Latin meaning "hinge"; hence all other virtues hinge on these — of courage, justice, temperance, and wisdom. Now all men were called to cultivate these virtues, but princes in particular were called to still others beyond these, such as princely magnanimity and liberality. These themes are developed in Cicero's *De Oficiis* or *On Duties*, and in Seneca's *On Clemency* and *On Benefits*.

The humanists anticipated the thesis Machiavelli would one day bring forth, namely that there ought to be a division between morality on the one hand and whatever happens to be expedient for the prince on the other. They answered it by cautioning that even if princely wickedness is not punished in this life, divine retribution in the next life would be fearsome and certain.

What made Machiavelli stand out so starkly was his radical departure from this traditional view of the prince's moral obligations. As the great Machiavelli scholar Quentin Skinner points out, "When we turn to *The Prince* we find this aspect of humanist morality suddenly and violently overturned."

The prince, says Machiavelli, must always "be prepared to act immorally when this becomes necessary." And "in order to maintain his power," he will — not just sometimes but often — be forced "to act treacherously, ruthlessly, and inhumanely."

Most people will never interact with the prince themselves, hence Machiavelli's note to the prince that "everyone can see what you appear to be" but "few have direct experience of what you really are." "A skillful deceiver," he continued, "always finds plenty of people who will let themselves be deceived." We can surmise from this what kind of person the prince would have to be.

It is customary to object at this point that Machiavelli counseled that the prince pursue virtue when possible, and that he should not pursue evil for its own sake. Machiavelli does indeed make such an argument in chapter 15 of *The Prince*. But on the other hand, Machiavelli says that conduct considered virtuous by traditional morality and the general run of mankind merely "seems virtuous," and that apparently wicked behavior that maintains one's power only seems vicious.

Skinner poses, and answers, the historian's natural question when faced with these moral claims:

> But what of the Christian objection that this is a foolish as well as a wicked position to adopt, since it forgets the day of judgment on which all injustices will finally be punished? About this Machiavelli says nothing at all. His silence is eloquent, indeed epoch-making; it echoed around Christian Europe, at first eliciting a stunned silence in return, and then a howl of execration that has never finally died away.

Machiavelli's view has sometimes been summarized as "the ends justify the means." Such a distillation does not capture all aspects of Machiavelli's thought, and no doubt this pithy summary irritates professors of political theory. But if the end in mind is the preservation of the prince's power, then "the ends justify the means" is not an unfair description of Machiavelli's counsel.

This principle, in turn, is what the collectivist State now appeals to in order to justify its own deviations from what people would otherwise consider moral and good. F.A. Hayek wrote,

> The principle that the end justifies the means is in individualist ethics regarded as the denial of all morals. In collectivist ethics it becomes necessarily the supreme rule; there is literally nothing which the consistent collectivist must not be prepared to do if it serves "the good of the whole," because the "good of the whole" is to him the only criterion of what ought to be done.

Collectivist ethics, he added, "knows no other limit than that set by expediency — the suitability of the particular act for the end in view."

Almost everyone now accepts, at least implicitly, the claim that a different set of moral rules applies to the State, or that to one degree or another the State is above morality as traditionally understood. Even if they would not use some of the verbal formulations of Machiavelli, at some level they believe it is unreasonable to expect the State or its functionaries to behave the way the rest of us do. The State may preserve itself by methods that no private business, or household, or organization, or individual would be allowed to employ for their own preservation. We accept this as normal.

So far, we seem driven toward anarchism. But let's look at another objection. What about democracy? Isn't the reason for bloated and tyrannical government the lack of genuine democratic control?

Hans Hoppe, in his great book *Democracy: The God That Failed* shows why this alleged "solution" won't work. In a democracy, the government will grab as much as it can, without regard to the future. Precisely because the holders of power do not own the government, they lack the incentive to look to the long run.

> A democratic ruler can use the government apparatus to his personal advantage, but he does not own it ... [h]e owns the current use of government resources, but not their capital value. In distinct contrast to a king, a president will want to maximize not total government wealth

(capital values and current income), but current income (regardless and at the expense of capital values).

Hoppe anticipates and dispatches an objection. If a democratic government acts as he indicates, will the people not remove it at the next election? The whole point of democracy, after all, is that seekers of power compete for the favor of the majority. Fear of removal will thus check the government's predation.

Unfortunately, as Hoppe notes, a democratic government can easily disable this "check" on it. The rulers buy votes by promising to the poor extravagant welfare benefits. The rich pay the price for these, but their dissatisfaction cannot overturn the government. They number but few compared with the poor whom the government enlists in its support. Thus predation proceeds unhindered, to the government's own advantage.

Hoppe's negative view of democracy has firm roots in the history of political thought. As he explains:

> The central task ahead of those wanting to turn the tide and prevent an outright breakdown is the "delegitimation" of the idea of democracy as the root cause of the present state of progressive "decivilization." To this purpose, one should first point out that it is difficult to find many proponents of democracy in the history of political theory. Almost all major thinkers had nothing but contempt for democracy. Even the Founding Fathers of the U.S., nowadays considered the model of a democracy, were strictly opposed to it. Without a single exception, they thought of democracy as nothing but mob-rule. They considered themselves to be members of a "natural aristocracy," and rather than a democracy they advocated an aristocratic republic. Furthermore, even among the few theoretical defenders of democracy such as Rousseau, for instance, it is almost impossible to find anyone advocating democracy for anything but extremely small communities (villages or towns). Indeed, in small communities where everyone knows everyone else personally most people cannot but acknowledge that the position of the 'haves' is typically based on their superior personal achievement just as the position of the 'have-nots' finds its typical explanation in their personal deficiencies and inferiority. Under these circumstances, it is far more difficult to get away with trying to loot other people and their personal property to one's advantage. In distinct contrast, in large territories encompassing millions or even hundreds of millions of people, where the potential looters do not know their victims, and

vice versa, the human desire to enrich oneself at another's expense is subject to little or no restraints.

More importantly, it must be made clear again that the idea of democracy is immoral as well as uneconomical. As for the moral status of majority rule, it must be pointed out that it allows for *A* and *B* to band together to rip off *C*, *C* and *A* in turn joining to rip off *B*, and then *B* and *C* conspiring against *A*, etc.

There is an even more fundamental objection to democracy. Suppose that we could overcome both problems: we could constrain the government to follow the will of the majority and we could prevent the majority from voting to despoil the rich. Democracy would still be a bad idea.

Even if the majority agrees to do something, what if you don't? Why should the majority have the power to force you to do what it commands? As Lysander Spooner well put it,

The principle that the majority have a right to rule the minority, practically resolves all government into a mere contest between two bodies of men, as to which of them shall be masters, and which of them slaves; a contest, that — however bloody — can, in the nature of things, never be finally closed, so long as man refuses to be a slave.

Each person properly has the right to rule over himself, a right no majority can override. As Rothbard explains,

the society of absolute self-ownership for all rests on the primordial fact of natural self-ownership by every man, and on the fact that each man may only live and prosper as he exercises his natural freedom of choice, adopts values, learns how to achieve them, etc. By virtue of being a man, he must use his mind to adopt ends and means; if someone aggresses against him to change his freely-selected course, this violates his nature; it violates the way he must function. In short, an aggressor interposes violence to thwart the natural course of a man's freely adopted ideas and values, and to thwart his actions based upon such values.

Once we accept this, we can see right away that no state, not even the most limited one, could be morally justified. The state gets its resources through taxation: it seizes our money and wealth. This is the whole point of the state. As the German sociologist Franz Oppenheimer long ago pointed out in *The State*,

There are two fundamentally opposed means whereby man, requiring sustenance, is impelled to obtain the necessary means for satisfying his desires. These are work and robbery, one's own labor and the forcible appropriation of the labor of others. Robbery! Forcible appropriation! These words convey to us ideas of crime and the penitentiary, since we are the contemporaries of a developed civilization, specifically based on the inviolability of property. And this tang is not lost when we are convinced that land and sea robbery is the primitive relation of life, just as the warriors' trade — which also for a long time is only organized mass robbery — constitutes the most respected of occupations. Both because of this, and also on account of the need of having, in the further development of this study, terse, clear, sharply opposing terms for these very important contrasts, I propose in the following discussion to call one's own labor and the equivalent exchange of one's own labor for the labor of others, the "economic means" for the satisfaction of needs, while the unrequited appropriation of the labor of others will be called the "political means."

Albert Jay Nock, Oppenheimer's chief American disciple and a founder of modern libertarianism, put the same point more pungently in his great book, *Our Enemy, the State*:

It is unfortunately none too well understood that, just as the State has no money of its own, so it has no power of its own. All the power it has is what society gives it, plus what it confiscates from time to time on one pretext or another; there is no other source from which State power can be drawn. Therefore every assumption of State power, whether by gift or seizure, leaves society with so much less power; there is never, nor can there be, any strengthening of State power without a corresponding and roughly equivalent depletion of social power. The general upshot of all this is that we see politicians of all schools and stripes behaving with the obscene depravity of degenerate children; like the loose-footed gangs that infest the railway-yards and purlieus of gas-houses, each group tries to circumvent another with respect to the fruit accruing to acts of public mischief.

7

How Would Anarchy Work?

DESPITE ALL THE PROBLEMS of the State, many of you are probably skeptical about anarchism. How would it work? We can't give an answer that gives all the details of the institutions of anarcho-capitalism, but we can sketch out some of its main features. Those who want a more detailed account should read Rothbard's *The Ethics of Liberty*.

Before we do so, we need to avoid a common mistake. Anarcho-capitalism means relying on the free market in everything; and we can't specify in advance exactly how the free market will work.

Leonard Read pointed out in a classic account that when something has been socialized, people jump to the conclusion that the market can't provide it:

> Imagine that our Federal government, at its very inception, had issued an edict that all boys and girls, from birth to adulthood, were to receive shoes and stockings from the federal government "for free." Next, imagine that this practice of "for free" shoes and stockings had been going on for lo, these 181 years! Lastly, imagine one of our contemporaries ... saying, "I do not believe that shoes and stockings for kids should be a government responsibility. ... This activity should never have been socialized. It is appropriately a free market activity. What, under these circumstances, would be the response to such a stated belief? Based on what we hear on every hand, once an activity has been socialized for a short time, the common chant would go like this, "Ah, but you would let the poor children go unshod."

Just for this reason, when you first mention anarchism to people, they will think it is impossible to put into practice. The basic idea, though, is very simple. People in an anarcho-capitalist society have rights. Each person owns himself and has the right to acquire and hold property. People accept a common law code that spells out these rights.

Now for the key point. People have the right of self-defense, but most of us can't do the job entirely by ourselves. We also need to settle disputes that involve the law code. In an anarcho-capitalist society, these functions would not be assigned to a monopoly agency that forced us to give money to it. Instead, people would purchase protection and judicial services on the market, just like other goods.

Rothbard spells out some of the details:

> Most likely, such services would be sold on an advance subscription basis, with premiums paid regularly and services to be supplied on call. Many competitors would undoubtedly arise, each attempting, by earning a reputation for efficiency and probity, to win a consumer market for its services. Of course, it is possible that in some areas a single agency would outcompete all others, but this does not seem likely when we realize that there is no territorial monopoly and that efficient firms would be able to open branches in other geographical areas. It seems likely, also, that supplies of police and judicial service would be provided by insurance companies, because it would be to their direct advantage to reduce the amount of crime as much as possible.

We know that the free market supplies goods and services far better than any alternative system. Why are protection and defense any different? Rothbard asked this question in 1949, and thinking about it made him an anarchist.

Why here do we face a unique situation in which provision by a coercive monopoly outperforms the market? The arguments for market provision of goods and services applied across the board. If so, should not even protection and defense be offered on the market rather than supplied by a coercive monopoly? Rothbard realized that he would either have to reject laissez-faire or embrace individualist anarchism. The decision, arrived at in the winter of 1949, was not difficult. Once the issue was raised, Rothbard realized that, however surprising it might seem, the free market need not be abandoned even here.

In arriving at his iconoclastic response, Rothbard was much influenced by several nineteenth-century individualist anarchists. He called Lysander Spooner's *No Treason* "the greatest case for anarchist political philosophy ever written," listing it under "Books That Formed Me." He termed Benjamin Tucker a "brilliant political philosopher" despite his "abysmal ignorance of economics." The detailed attempt by the Belgian economist Gustave de Molinari to spell out how a system of private protection would work impressed him:

> In short, he reasoned: [if] free competition [can] supply consumers with the most efficient service, and monopoly was always bad in all other goods and services, why should this not apply to the service of defense. He maintained that single entrepreneurs would be able to supply protection in the rural districts, while large insurance type companies could supply the urban consumers.

What are the advantages of this system? For one thing, we no longer have a predatory body that seizes money from the rest of us. There is no longer a division between producers — taxpayers — and predators — tax consumers. The protection agencies make their money in the same way any other business on the free market does: by selling its product to consumers.

Because of this, we eliminate the main problem that plagued "limited government." This problem was that no matter how carefully the limits were put in place in a constitution, we are relying on the government — a monopoly agency — to police itself. Here we don't face this difficulty. Protection agencies are in competition with each other. If an agency tried to grab power in the way a government does, its clients would shift to a competing agency that offered better terms.

As always, Rothbard explains the issue with unmatched clarity:

> Another common objection to the workability of free-market defense wonders: May not one or more of the defense agencies turn its coercive power to criminal uses? In short, may not a private police agency use its force to aggress against others, or may not a private court collude to make fraudulent decisions and thus aggress against its subscribers and victims? It is very generally assumed that those who postulate a stateless society are also naïve enough to believe that, in such a society, all men would be "good," and no one would wish to aggress against his

neighbor. There is no need to assume any such magical or miraculous change in human nature. Of course, some of the private defense agencies will become criminal, just as some people become criminal now. But the point is that in a stateless society there would be no regular, legalized channel for crime and aggression, no government apparatus the control of which provides a secure monopoly for invasion of person and property. When a State exists, there does exist such a built-in channel, namely, the coercive taxation power, and the compulsory monopoly of forcible protection. In the purely free-market society, a would-be criminal police or judiciary would find it very difficult to take power, since there would be no organized State apparatus to seize and use as the instrumentality of command. To create such an instrumentality *de novo* is very difficult, and, indeed, almost impossible; historically, it took State rulers centuries to establish a functioning State apparatus. Furthermore, the purely free-market, stateless society would contain within itself a system of built-in "checks and balances" that would make it almost impossible for such organized crime to succeed. There has been much talk about "checks and balances" in the American system, but these can scarcely be considered checks at all, since every one of these institutions is an agency of the central government and eventually of the ruling party of that government. The checks and balances in the stateless society consist precisely in the free market, i.e., the existence of freely competitive police and judicial agencies that could quickly be mobilized to put down any outlaw agency.

It is true that there can be no absolute guarantee that a purely market society would not fall prey to organized criminality. But this concept is far more workable than the truly Utopian idea of a strictly limited government, an idea that has never worked historically. And understandably so, for the State's built-in monopoly of aggression and inherent absence of free-market checks has enabled it to burst easily any bonds that well-meaning people have tried to place upon it. Finally, the worst that could possibly happen would be for the State to be reestablished. And since the State is what we have now, any experimentation with a stateless society would have nothing to lose and everything to gain.

You might wonder, though, wouldn't there be big problems if people in a dispute belonged to competing agencies? In America today, we live under a single legal system — although it's one the government often abuses, as we've seen. Isn't this a big advantage that would be lost in an anarchist society?

No, it isn't. Competing agencies would find in very much in their interest to reach an agreement about what to do in such cases. If you sued someone in your agency's courts and he got a different verdict from his agency, an appeals court would decide the matter. Each agency would use the common libertarian law code, so coming up with an acceptable decision wouldn't be hard.

Once more, Rothbard is our guide:

> The two courts, each subscribed to by one of the two parties, have split their verdicts. In that case, the two courts will submit the case to an appeals court, or arbitrator, which the two courts agree upon. There seems to be no real difficulty about the concept of an appeals court. As in the case of arbitration contracts, it seems very likely that the various private courts in the society will have prior agreements to submit their disputes to a particular appeals court. How will the appeals judges be chosen? Again, as in the case of arbitrators or of the first judges on the free market, they will be chosen for their expertise and their reputation for efficiency, honesty, and integrity. Obviously, appeals judges who are inefficient or biased will scarcely be chosen by courts who will have a dispute. The point here is that there is no need for a legally established or institutionalized single, monopoly appeals court system, as states now provide. There is no reason why there cannot arise a multitude of efficient and honest appeals judges who will be selected by the disputant courts, just as there are numerous private arbitrators on the market today. The appeals court renders its decision, and the courts proceed to enforce it. ... No society can have unlimited judicial appeals, for in that case there would be no point to having judges or courts at all. Therefore, every society, whether statist or anarchist, will have to have some socially accepted cutoff point for trials and appeals. My suggestion is the rule that the agreement *of any two courts*, be decisive. "Two" is not an arbitrary figure, for it reflects the fact that there are two parties, the plaintiff and the defendant, to any alleged crime or contract dispute.

What about the libertarian code? This is the other key tool that, together with the competing protection agencies, eliminates all the problems caused by the Leviathan State which we have discussed earlier in the book. How does it do this? It radically restricts the scope of laws. There are, e.g., no drug laws, gun control laws, or laws regulating "capitalist acts between consenting adults." There is no danger of an aggressive or imperialist foreign policy, because there is no foreign policy. Each protection agency is confined to protecting its clients. Agencies, or allied groups of agencies, would defend against an organized invasion; but, once more, there is no foreign policy as we know it.

Why is the law code limited in this drastic way? The basic idea is simple. We start with two commonsense ideas that are difficult to dispute. First, every person is a self-owner. This means that you make all decisions about your own body. No state, for example, can draft you into the army because you, and no one else, have jurisdiction over your body. No one can override your right over your own body by saying that some other people, or "society," need your body or your labor more than you do.

Rothbard spells this out:

> the society of absolute self-ownership for all rests on the primordial fact of natural self-ownership by every man, and on the fact that each man may only live and prosper as he exercises his natural freedom of choice, adopts values, learns how to achieve them, etc. By virtue of being a man, he must use his mind to adopt ends and means; if someone aggresses against him to change his freely-selected course, this violates his nature; it violates the way he must function. In short, an aggressor interposes violence to thwart the natural course of a man's freely adopted ideas and values, and to thwart his actions based upon such values.

We need only one other assumption to derive the basic parts of the libertarian law code. This is that all resources start out without ownership claims. People have to do something to acquire property. People aren't entitled to a share of the world's resources just by being born.

How then can people acquire property? Once they get it, it's easy to see how they can pass it on to other people. They can do this by trading with others or by gifts to them. But if you ask someone, "How did you get your property?," and he answers by telling you he got it from someone else, the same question would come up for that person. Eventually, you would come to someone who didn't get the property from someone else. Where did he get it from?

We already have what we need to answer this question. If you own yourself, and the earth starts off free of ownership claims, then you are free to fence off a certain area and claim it as your own. How much can you claim? What exactly do have to do to the unowned land to make it your permanent property? The answers to these questions can't be entirely fixed in advance. They depend in part on what people in particular communities find acceptable. But the general principle is clear. You get property initially by homesteading it.

Once again, Rothbard explains the issue clearly:

> Crusoe finds virgin, unused land on the island; land, in short, unused and uncontrolled by anyone, and hence *unowned*. By finding land resources, by learning how to use them, and, in particular, by actually *transforming* them into a more useful shape, Crusoe has, in the memorable phrase of John Locke, "mixed his labor with the soil." In doing so, in stamping the imprint of his personality and his energy on the land, he has naturally converted the land and its fruits into his *property*. Hence, the isolated man *owns* what he *uses* and *transforms*; therefore, in his case there is no problem of what *should be A's* property as against *B's*. Any man's property is *ipso facto* what he *produces*, i.e., what he transforms into use by his own effort. His property in land and capital goods continues down the various stages of production, until Crusoe comes to *own* the consumer goods which he has produced, until they finally disappear through his consumption of them.

> As long as an individual remains isolated, then, there is no problem whatever about how far his *property* — his ownership — extends; as a rational being with free will, it extends over his own body, and it extends further over the material goods which he transforms with his labor. Suppose that Crusoe had landed not on a small island, but on a new and virgin continent, and that, standing on the shore, he had claimed "ownership" of the entire new continent by virtue of his prior discovery. This assertion would be sheer empty vainglory, so long as no one else came upon the continent. For the *natural fact* is that his true property — his *actual control* over material goods — would extend only so far as his actual labor brought them into production. His true ownership could not extend beyond the power of his own reach. Similarly, it would be empty and meaningless for Crusoe to trumpet that he does not "really" own some or all of what he has produced (perhaps this Crusoe happens to be a romantic opponent of the property concept), for in fact the use and *therefore* the ownership has already been his. Crusoe, in natural fact, owns his own self and the extension of his self into the material world, neither more nor less.

Individuals in isolation, then, can acquire property; and things don't change when more people enter the scene. As we said before, all we need to add is an agreement among the people in a community on the principle of acquisition.

We could go on at greater length about the libertarian law code, but for our purposes, there is no need to do so. Once we have self-ownership and property rights, that's all we need. Individuals are then free to make whatever exchanges they wish. This is the basis on which the free market can get started.

Before we leave the libertarian law code, one issue requires mention. What about IP? (Intellectual property, i.e., patents, copyrights, trademarks, etc.)? For some people, this has become a central topic in libertarianism. Rothbard didn't regard it that way: it's an issue worthy of attention, no doubt, but not a crux of his whole position.

His views on the topic have stood the test of time: despite talk to the contrary, there has been no "revolution" in libertarian thinking on IP. In essence, Rothbard relied on contract. Inventors and creators are entitled to whatever protection for their creations they can get by contract, no less and no more.

> We have seen ... that the acid test by which we judge whether or not a certain practice or law is or is not consonant with the free market is this: Is the outlawed practice implicit or explicit theft? If it is, then the free market would outlaw it; if not, then its outlawry is itself government interference in the free market. Let us consider copyright. A man writes a book or composes music. When he publishes the book or sheet of music, he imprints on the first page the word "copyright." This indicates that any man who agrees to purchase this product also agrees as part of the exchange *not* to recopy or reproduce this work for sale. In other words, the author does not sell his property outright to the buyer; he sells it *on condition* that the buyer not reproduce it for sale. Since the buyer does not buy the property outright, but only on this condition, any infringement of the contract by him or a subsequent buyer is *implicit theft* and would be treated accordingly on the free market. The copyright is therefore a logical device of property right on the free market.

> Part of the patent protection now obtained by an inventor could be achieved on the free market by a type of "copyright" protection.

Thus, inventors must now *mark* their machines as being patented. The mark puts the buyers on notice that the invention is patented and that they cannot sell that article. But the same could be done to extend the copyright system, and without patent. In the purely free market, the inventor could mark his machine *copyright*, and then anyone who buys the machine buys it *on the condition* that he will not reproduce and sell such a machine for profit. Any violation of this contract would constitute implicit theft and be prosecuted accordingly on the free market.

The patent is incompatible with the free market *precisely to the extent that it goes beyond the copyright*. The man who has not bought a machine and who arrives at the same invention independently, will, on the free market, be perfectly able to use and sell his invention. Patents prevent a man from using his invention even though all the property is his and he has not stolen the invention, either explicitly or implicitly, from the first inventor. Patents, therefore, are grants of exclusive monopoly privilege by the State and are *invasive* of property rights on the market.

The crucial distinction between patents and copyrights, then, is not that one is mechanical and the other literary. The fact that they have been applied that way is an historical accident and does not reveal the critical difference between them. The crucial difference is that copyright is a logical attribute of property right on the free market, while patent is a monopoly invasion of that right.

We now know enough to see how anarchism would get rid of the terrible problems, discussed in earlier chapters of this book, which the State has created. We wouldn't have an aggressive foreign policy, because there wouldn't be a foreign policy at all. There is no scope for one: the nearest equivalent would be the agreements on appeals procedures among the protection agencies. There would be no government to regulate drugs, keep us under surveillance, suppress our liberty or impose foolish and anti-human environmental regulations on us. The Fed would not exist. Money would be entirely supplied by the free market.

Because of the crucial importance of money, let's examine in more detail what a free market money supply would look like. Money would not consist of pieces of paper, which the State forces us to accept as legal tender. Rather, money would be a commodity, in all probability gold.

As Murray Rothbard emphasized, the essence of the gold standard is that it puts power in the hands of the people. They are no longer dependent on the whims of central bankers, treasury officials, and high rollers in money centers. Money becomes not merely an accounting device but a real form of property like any other. It is secure, portable, universally valued, and rather than falling in value, it maintains or rises in value over time. Under a real gold standard, there is no need for a central bank, and banks themselves become like any other business, not some gigantic socialistic operation sustained by trillions in public money.

Imagine holding money and watching it grow rather than shrink in its purchasing power in terms of goods and services. That's what life is like under gold. Savers are rewarded rather than punished. No one uses the monetary system to rob anyone else. The government can only spend what it has and no more. Trade across borders is not thrown into constant upheaval because of a change in currency valuations.

Readers should now have a good understanding of the basics of anarchism, and it should be apparent why this system is better than the State. Sometimes, issues just are black and white: Free market anarchism is good and the State is evil.

But even if we are right that there is a strong moral case for anarchism, we need to confront an important objection. But defense is supposed to be different. We all want it. But something in the nature of things is said to prevent us from organizing it ourselves. We need government to do it because defense is a "public good," something the market can't provide for a variety of convoluted reasons (free rider problems, non-excludability, high cost, etc.). It is believed that we would rather be taxed to have bureaucrats defend us. This belief is held across the political spectrum. The arguments about defense and security and military budgets never go to the core.

What if the conventional theory is wrong? What if it turns out that the private sector can provide national defense, not in the sense of contracting with private companies to build bombs at taxpayer expense, but really provide it to paying customers at a profit? The argument of an explosive book edited by Hans-Hermann Hoppe and published by the Mises Institute, is precisely that it can. If you have never before considered the idea, or considered it but wondered if you were crazy, you need to read *The Myth of National Defense*.

In the entire history of economic and political ideas, you can find only a handful of writings that argue along these lines, and nothing that makes the argument in this level of detail or with this level of theoretical and practical rigor. This volume is the best proof I've seen in years that intellectuals can perform essential services to society: shattering myths, causing a complete rethinking of widely held fallacies, assembling historical evidence in patterns that reveal certain theoretical truths, and making obvious the previously unthinkable.

The bias in favor of government provision of defense, and the taboo about other alternatives, has been, of course, entrenched, for hundreds, even thousands, of years. And certainly since Hobbes, just about every political philosopher has conjured up nightmare scenarios about the consequences of life without government defense, while ignoring the reality of the actual nightmare of government provision. As Hoppe writes, "the first person to provide a systematic explanation for the apparent failure of governments as security producers" was nineteenth century thinker Gustave de Molinari. In our own time, the only people doing serious work on this subject, perhaps the most important of our time, are the Austro-libertarians."

Government failure, yes, but private defense? Before you say this is an outlandish idea, remember that just about everything else done in the private sector sounds, at some level, implausible. What if I told you that oil needs to be extracted from the house, on demand and at the price of bottled water?

It seems impossible. The first impulse might be to say that we need a government program to manage such a thing, but the non-intuitive reality is that government could never do such a thing on its own. Only the private sector can manage to coordinate the thousands of processes essential to such an undertaking.

Hoppe begins his argument with a quotation from Jefferson's Declaration of Independence. The British government had failed to protect the lives and liberties of the citizens of the colonies, and so it was the natural, God-given right (the Declaration argued) of the people to throw off that government and "provide new guards for their future security."

Not much has changed in the intervening years, Hoppe says, because today the US is not protecting the lives and liberties of Americans and thus it is our right to provide new guards. The remainder of the book explores how such guards can come about.

Hoppe draws attention to the core problem of orthodox defense theory. The presumption on the part of nearly everyone is that monopoly is a bad thing. It is inefficient. It robs society of the benefits of competition. It limits choice. It places too much power in the hands of producers and not enough in the hands of consumers. The second presumption is that defense must be provided by a monopoly. Philosophers and economists have long presumed that the first argument about monopoly is false when applied to defense, and so it must be thrown out. This book takes the reverse view: the first argument is true and the second one is false.

He goes further. He says that there is no way to make a government monopoly of any kind work well. Government cannot be limited once it is conceded that it must be the sole provider of defense. It will continue to raise the price of the "service" as it provides less and less. Democracy doesn't help, says Hoppe. Democracy is as likely to be as war-like and crushing of internal dissent as the total state (see, e.g., the American Civil War).

Readers might still hesitate. Anarchism may sound good in theory, but what realistic chance do we have to establish it? Isn't it a Utopian pipe-dream?

To view matters this way would be to give up before we started. What we need to realize is that the State system is dead. It cannot sustain itself, and we must be ready when it falls with something better.

The State as we've known it — and that includes its political parties and its redistributionary, military, regulatory, and money-creating bureaucracies — just can't get it together. It's as true now as it has been for some 20 years: the Nation-State is in precipitous decline. Once imbued with grandeur and majesty, personified by its Superman powers to accomplish amazing global feats, it is now a wreck and out of ideas.

It doesn't seem that way because the State is more in-your-face than it has been in all of American history. We see the State at the airport with the incompetent bullying ways of the TSA. We see it in the ridiculous dinosaur of the post office, forever begging for more money so it can continue to do things the way it did them in 1950. We see it in the federalized cops in our towns, once seen as public servants but now revealed as what they have always been: armed tax collectors, censors, spies, thugs.

These are themselves marks of decline. The mask of the State is off. And it has been off for such a long time that we can hardly remember what it looked like when it was on.

So let's take a quick tour. If you live in a big metropolitan city, drive to the downtown post office (if it is still standing). There you will find a remarkable piece of architecture, tall and majestic and filled with grandeur. There is a liberal use of Roman-style columns. The ceilings indoors are extremely high and thrilling. It might even be the biggest and most impressive building around.

This is a building of an institution that believed in itself. After all, this was the institution that carried the mail, which was the only way that people had to communicate with each other when most of these places were first erected. The state took great pride in offering this service, which it held up as being superior to anything the market could ever provide (even if market provisions like the Pony Express had to be outlawed). Postmen were legendary (or so we were told) for their willingness to brave the elements to bring us the essential thing we needed in life apart from food, clothing, and shelter.

And today? Look at the thing that we call the post office. It is a complete wreck, a national joke, a hanger-on from a day long gone. They deliver physical spam to our mail boxes, and a few worthwhile things every once in a while, but the only time they are in the news is when we hear another report of their bankruptcy and need for a bailout.

It's the same with all the grand monuments of yesteryear's statism. Think of the Hoover Dam, Mount Rushmore, the endless infrastructure projects of the New Deal, the Eisenhower interstate highway system, the moon shot, the sprawling monuments to itself that the State has erected from sea to shining sea. These all came about in an age when the only real alternative to socialism was considered to be fascism. This was an age when freedom — as in the old-fashioned sense — was just out of the question.

The State in all times and all places operates by force — and force alone. But the style of rule changes. The fascist style emphasized inspiration, magnificence, industrial progress, grandeur, all headed by a valiant leader making smart decisions about all things. This style of American rule lasted from the New Deal through the end of the Cold War.

But this whole system of inspiration has nearly died out. In the communist tradition of naming the stages of history, we can call this late fascism. The fascist system in the end cannot work because, despite the claims, the State does not have the means to achieve what it promises. It does not possess the capability to outrun private markets in technology, of serving the population in the way markets can, of making things more plentiful or cheaper, or even of providing basic services in a manner that is economically efficient.

Fascism, like socialism, cannot achieve its aims. So there is a way in which it makes sense to speak of a stage of history: We are in the stage of late fascism. The grandeur is gone, and all we are left with is a gun pointed at our heads. The system was created to be great, but it is reduced in our time to being crude. Valor is now violence. Majesty is now malice.

Consider whether there is any national political leader in power today the death of whom would call forth anywhere near the same level of mourning as the death of Steve Jobs. People know in their hearts who serves them, and it is not the guy with jack boots, tasers on his belt, and a federal badge. The time when we looked to this man as a public servant is long gone. And this reality only speeds the inevitable death of the State as the twentieth century re-invented it.

Free market anarchists of all countries, unite: We have a world to win!

FURTHER READING

ANYONE WANTING TO LEARN more about anarcho-capitalism could do no better than to begin with two books by Murray Rothbard, *For a New Liberty* and *The Ethics of Liberty*. The first of these diagnoses what is wrong with the regime of state domination: the second describes in substantial detail how the anarchist alternative would work. (For that matter, anything written by Rothbard is highly recommended.) Hans-Hermann Hoppe has edited a collection, *The Myth of National Defense*, which refutes the myth that an anarchist society could not adequately defend itself.

For more detail on the fascist character of the present American regime, see my *Fascism vs. Capitalism*. John T. Flynn's World War II classic *As We Go Marching* has not lost its relevance. Readers will find an excellent account of the war system and the history of American foreign policy in a book by the great historian Ralph Raico, *Great Wars and Great Leaders: A Libertarian Rebuttal*. Raico's *Classical Liberalism and the Austrian School* should not be missed. Tom DiLorenzo's *The Real Lincoln* is vital for understanding the growth of the State during the War Between the States, and for its skeptical account of Abraham Lincoln, a false god promoted by the State's propagandists. Robert Higgs ties together the war system and the growth of the State in his monumental *Crisis and Leviathan*.

Ron Paul has been the foremost opponent of the Fed in Congress, and his *The Case for Gold* explains what a free market money system would be like. Murray Rothbard's *What Has Government Done to Our Money?* is indispensable.

Ludwig von Mises definitely refuted socialism and interventionism in *Socialism*. Mises's analysis of fascism as a form of socialism in *Planning for Freedom* underlies the treatment of fascism in this book. Hans Hoppe's *A Theory of Socialism and Capitalism* argues that all interference with the free market is in reality a form of socialism.

Finally, everybody should read two classics of libertarian anarchism: Franz Oppenheimer, *The State* and Albert Jay Nock, *Our Enemy, the State*.

INDEX